SHERLOCK HOLMES in *Portrait and Profile*

WALTER KLINEFELTER, a retired schoolteacher, is the author of *A Small Display of Old Maps and Plans, Maps in Miniature, Illustrations in Miniature, The World Minutely Mapped, Christmas Books* and other bibliographies, *The Fortsas Bibliohoax, Catalogue of Choice Books Found by Pantagruel in the Library of Saint Victor,* and *Ex Libris A. Conan Doyle: Sherlock Holmes,* a study of the sources of the Holmes stories.

SHERLOCK HOLMES *in* Portrait and Profile

WALTER KLINEFELTER

With an introduction by VINCENT STARRETT

1963   *Syracuse University Press*

Library of Congress Catalog Card: 63-19727

THIS BOOK HAS BEEN PUBLISHED WITH THE
ASSISTANCE OF A FORD FOUNDATION GRANT.

Set in Linotype Caslon by The Heffernan Press Inc., Worcester, Mass. Presswork by Halliday Lithograph Corporation, West Hanover, Mass. Bound by Vail-Ballou Press, Binghamton, N. Y. Designed by Freeman Champney. Jacket design by Richard G. Underwood.

Manufactured in the United States of America

Acknowledgments

ACKNOWLEDGMENTS of valuable assistance are gratefully made to Vincent Starrett, John R. Hetherington, Jay Finley Christ, Ellery Queen, and to the reference librarians of many of the major public libraries of the United States. The manuscript of this book was read by the late Edgar W. Smith, Sherlockian extraordinary and founder of *The Baker Street Journal,* whose consummate knowledge of the canon enabled him to detect a few errors, which have been corrected. The Frederic Dorr Steele drawings reproduced herein appear with the kind permission of Mrs. Mary Steele; Robert M. Hoof's drawing is used by courtesy of *The Courier-Journal,* Louisville, Kentucky, and G. Patrick Nelson's by leave of the editor of *Cosmopolitan.* All other illustrations reproduced are in the public domain.

Introduction

WHAT does a murderer look like? Does anybody know?

Did Lombroso know? He believed that by observing the facial angle, or measuring the cranium, or something like that, it was possible to distinguish a citizen predisposed to crime. But the warden of a famous reformatory once assured the late Edmund Pearson that every facial characteristic, every skull measurement, to be found in a penal institution could be duplicated in any state legislature in the nation.

There would appear to be no certain way of telling a potential criminal; but there is one thing *everybody* knows—you and I and the man in the street, the schoolboy and the college president, the bus conductor and the millionaire on his yacht. We all know what a detective looks like. He looks like Sherlock Holmes.

And what does Sherlock Holmes look like? We know what he looked like to Dr. Watson; but do we know how he appeared to Mrs. Hudson? We can guess what he looked like to Scotland Yard. Professor Moriarty, visiting him, found less frontal development than he had expected; but Dr. Mortimer, who coveted his skull, was gratified by the detective's well-marked supraorbital development. For thousands of his admirers he is any man in a deerstalker hat, smoking a curved pipe; yet Holmes did not always wear a deerstalker, and the curve is uncanonical.

Currently, no doubt, the picture of Sherlock Holmes in most minds is that of Basil Rathbone; but it was not always so—once it was the portrait of William Gillette. The evolution of that famous profile is a story in itself, the story of the detective's illustrators no less than his impersonators. It is that story Walter Klinefelter tells in his delightful book.

I am happy to introduce Mr. Klinefelter's monograph on the iconography of Sherlock Holmes, a pleasing addition to the mounting number of books in praise of the world's best loved and best documented detective. Its scholarship is evident; but, scholarship aside, it is an enchanting picture-book and a fascinating research that admirers of the Master on all levels will hail with satisfaction. Collectors, to be sure, are going to have a difficult time finding those old issues of the *Baltimore Weekly Sun*, the *Boston Daily Traveler*, the *Chicago Inter Ocean*, and other early newspaper appearances described by Mr. Klinefelter; but one envies them their quest. No collection of Sherlock Holmes ever will be complete; but half of the fun is in the search.

Surely the highest tribute to the historicity of Sherlock Holmes is the impressive volume of writings devoted to his private life no less than to his public career; essays in fantastic scholarship, solemn tongue-in-cheek fooling in the fields of textual criticism and imaginary biography. Surely the whole phenomenon is one of the most delightful chapters of literary chronicle. It has been remarked that the civilized inhabitants of our planet who are strangers to the face and fame of Sherlock Holmes are probably less numerous than the stones left unturned in the gardens of detective literature. As to his fame, there is no doubt whatever. As to the familiar features: in the pages that follow, Mr. Klinefelter tells how they came to be familiar—and reveals some early likenesses that may astonish even initiates.

One has nothing to add to his revelations; but it is an uneasy reflection that Holmes began to influence native writers in China as early as the eighteen-nineties. His name, by a curious corruption of sounds, became *Fu-erh-mo-hsi*; and his adventures with ghosts, fox-women, tiger-men, and other supernatural monsters, might well curl the eyebrows of Baker Street specialists. It would be interesting some day to see a portrait of *Fu-erh-mo-hsi,* of the right period, if one can be found.

VINCENT STARRETT

Contents

Portrait and Profile

SHERLOCK HOLMES in *Portrait and Profile*

THE WRITINGS which comprise the published history of Mr. Sherlock Holmes are in more ways than one a peculiar body of literary work. Long recognized as the most acceptable of the latter-day revelations in their *genre,* they have attracted a host of ardent readers in every clime and country of this planet, to the greater number of whom their perusal has always served to impart a state of the highest felicity. At the same time these writings have also been to some of their closest students and most devoted admirers a source of no little exasperation, mainly because as revelation they fall somewhat short of much desired definitiveness, not merely with regard to the many unrecorded cases, but also as concerns the first two decades of Holmes' life. Then, too, in taking such form as they may be said to have assumed for the most part from the order of their publication, they are marked by a notable lack of chronological sequence. And as if these circumstances were not in themselves sufficient cause for vexation to those who would know all about the immortal detective, the various sections of the canon, in the course of their initial magazine, newspaper, and book publications, received illustrative treatment at the hands of quite a number of artists, no two of whom seem to have perceived or visualized the same Sherlock Holmes.

The Holmesian portraiture that resulted was of a kind that does not lend itself readily to review in the form generally employed in pictorial or photographic biographies. Therefore, that which follows is more or less a story-by-story or book-by-book account of what the detective's various portrayers made of him as the piecemeal records of his cases were inconsecutively released.

The student well advanced in *Sherlockismus* is aware, of course, that the earliest portrait of the detective now extant was not executed in oil, or crayon, or any of the other *media* artists use for pictorial representation, but was done in words, and by a word-painter of no mean talent. It is an arresting depiction, this sketch from life in black on white by the estimable John H. Watson, M.D., late of the Army Medical Department:

"His very person and appearance were such as to strike the attention of the most casual observer. In height he was rather over six feet, and so excessively lean that he seemed to be considerably taller. His eyes were sharp and piercing, . . . and his thin hawk-like nose gave his whole expression an air of alertness and decision. His chin, too, had the prominence and squareness which mark the man of decision."[1]

Thus was our beloved Sherlock featured forth as Watson saw him in the early days of their association, when both were in their late twenties.[2] The bold, free strokes that go to make up the portrait are few in number, yet the composition is essentially complete. Its author afterwards oft saw Sherlock plain, in varying moods and under diverse conditions, at home in Baker Street and abroad upon the chase, but he never had to change the groundwork of his picture in any really important particular. He merely added, when occasion offered or required, certain heightening touches here and there to accentuate this feature or that, as when he stressed the highly notable beakiness of nose that contributed to give Holmes a definitely Amerind-like cast of countenance,[3] or brought out the extremely dolichocephalic shape and the well-marked frontal development of his head,[4] or sketched in some one of those many now familiar details that delight the true Sherlockophile but do not actually alter the fundamentals of this first presentment of the great detective.

Watson's word-picture of Holmes as he looked in 1881 had already had publication in "a small brochure, with the somewhat fantastic title of 'A Study in Scarlet,' "[5] when the curious arrangement was concluded with Arthur Conan Doyle, assumably at some time early in the year 1886, whereby the latter was granted permission to publish the tale under his own name and to use the same title originally given it by Watson. How Doyle eventually sold Watson's first Holmesian revelation down the river to Ward, Lock & Company, publishers of The Select Library of Fiction and *Beeton's Christmas Annual,* is a well-known story and does not call for retelling here. Sherlock then was well on his way to making his name as famous as he knew, even from the earliest days of his association with Watson, that he had it in himself to make it. Though his pictures had not yet begun to appear in the newspapers,[6] he had already caught a sizable segment of the public eye, having distinguished himself in a number of highly sensational cases, among them some of his most successful ones.[7] Watson never got around to inditing complete accounts of all of them, and those he did write up in the form in which the reading public now knows them still remained unpublished at that time, but their main details must have been much more than mere hearsay at Scotland Yard and in the inner offices of the larger newspapers. In fact, for a number of years the public prints had been giving rather extended notices of the more out-of-the-ordinary of Holmes' cases.[8]

Book publishers, however, do not seem to have heard much of him. At least, it is evident that the purchasers of *A Study in Scarlet* set no high literary value on the work, for they did not risk putting Sherlock in a book by himself. Instead, they made him the leader in the aforementioned *Beeton's Annual* for 1887, and to provide the major embellishments for the tale they chose D. H. Friston, an illustrator of some note in those days. Friston furnished four drawings, of which two picture Holmes, but of those two only one provides an over-all view of him.

It has been said of this portrait that it is a cause for acute distress to the great detective's more ardent admirers. The Holmes it pictures is indeed something "to strike the attention of the most casual observer," for Friston gave him luxuriant sideburns, garbed him in a voluminous greatcoat fitted with an enormous cape, and on his head placed a hat that is neither an out-and-out billycock nor yet a fireman's helmet, but looks rather like the sort of hybrid piece of headgear that might be expected to eventuate from an illicit union of the two, if anything like that were possible. Even so, the result is less a travesty of person than of appearance. If Friston's conception of the detective were to be shorn of the outlandish sidewhiskers, divested of the capacious overcoat, and relieved of the gaudy chapeau, a not too impossible Holmes in profile probably would stand forth. And if a deerstalker were then to be placed on his head, he might not prove so utterly distressing after all. In Friston's portrait he is not quite so lean as Watson saw him. He has the correct height, however,[9] and the designated squareness of chin; and there is a pronounced aquilinity of feature too, not high-beaked Amerind, but of a sort rather more like that which characterizes certain Mediterranean types. (The picture appears overleaf.)

That Friston drew his Holmes from the living original,

or even from any remembered glimpses of his actual person, is hardly believable, for there is not the faintest reflection here of that "certain quiet primness of dress" which Holmes affected.[10] It seems much more likely that the artist made what he considered to be a fairly close pictorial study of Watson's description, which he then dressed up with sartorial, whiskerish, and sundry other effects after his own fancy.

Conan Doyle had sold Watson's *Study in Scarlet* down the river, but not so far down that he lost all control over its destiny. How else could one account for the fact that when Ward, Lock & Company brought out the work separately in

1888 it was Charles Doyle, the father of Conan, who supplied the embellishments? In view of the son's connection with Dr. Watson, this would seem to have been the happiest choice that could have been made from all available illustrators. One likes to imagine that, once the assignment was definitely agreed upon, the elder Doyle hurried off without delay to Baker Street, for if access to the menage at 221B was to be had by any artist, here surely was one who needed only to ask in order to have his wish fulfilled. Of course, Holmes pretended to bridle a bit at the idea of sitting for the execution of his likeness, a piece of acting that no doubt proved to be the most unconvincing one of his entire career. But a request for permission to make a sketch of him would take him in the weakest point of his armor, which was rather more than a mere tinge of vanity, and, naturally, he could not have kept up a pretense of displeasure for long. When he had done then with his sham grousing, everything was very easily arranged for his definitive delineation. That is what one likes to imagine as having taken place. Alas, what really happened is rudely disillusioning, for not one of the things that have been imagined seems to have suggested itself to the minds of any of the persons immediately interested, not even to the mind of the artist, who should have been the one person, after Holmes, most closely concerned.

Charles Doyle's illustrations were six in number. In three of them there are three different conceptions of Sherlock Holmes, which, to put it as charitably as any well-disposed person could, are the veriest of counterfeit presentments. The most cursory glance at the first one (page 6), which is a pictorial interpretation of the detective as he was standing just inside the door of the room in which the dead body of Enoch Drebber lies, reveals the fact that there is nothing remotely resembling any detail of Watson's description of his friend to be recognized in a single feature of this figure with its narrow, sloping shoulders and its broad-browed, dissipated-looking face which has only the suggestion of a nose, and that on the *retroussé* side rather than the hawk-like. The nonchalance of Holmes' pose in the presence of horrific death as pictured by Doyle on Drebber's face contrasts very markedly with a ludicrously bonneted Watson's conventional attitude of reverence and a decidedly unferretlike Lestrade's expression of sheer cock-eyed horror.

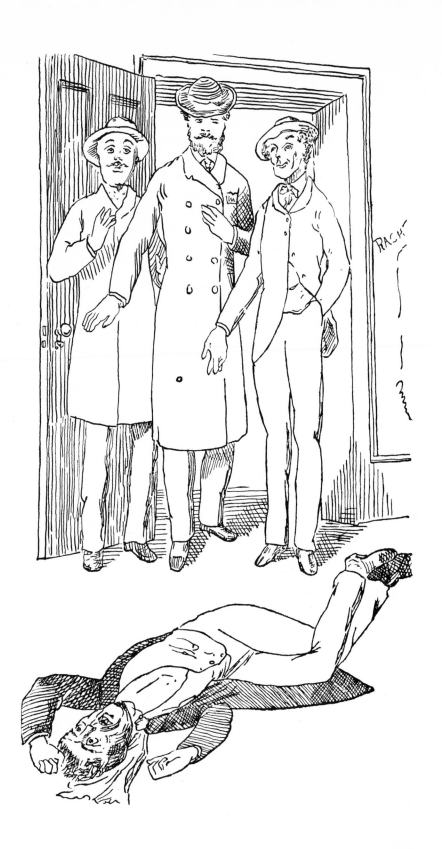

SHERLOCK HOLMES in

Charles Doyle's second attempt at a picturization of Holmes (this is not reproduced here) shows the old woman[11] calling for the ring lost by Jefferson Hope. Seated at his desk, the detective presents a physiognomy that has some points of similarity to the one shown in the first illustration but looks even more dissipated—somewhat as one might imagine Edgar Allan Poe to have looked on a morning after an especially lurid night before.

In the third representation Charles Doyle definitely achieved the all-time low in the portraiture of the man. Mere words are too ineffectual to describe this Holmes. An arrival at any adequate conception of what the artist made of him is possible only through an actual look (above) at the staring-eyed, weak-mouthed person in schoolmasterish attitude calling to attention five of the original members of the unofficial Baker Street detective police, or, as they were more familiarly known, the Baker Street Irregulars, whose portraiture, incidentally, is the best part of the illustration.

Charles Doyle failed to get the sixth member of the Irregulars into the picture, and the omission is a regrettable one, for there is something uncannily psychic about his rather too grown-up representations of these "street Arabs" standing at left-handed salute. Reading in the usual order, the faces of the first three, which support hirsute adornment quite advanced for their supposed years, unquestionably are prefigurative portrayals of a like number of the better-known bearded men who have been members of the present-day Baker Street Irregulars; namely, Fletcher Pratt, Christopher Morley, and Rex Stout.[12] At present the fourth, a sad-faced lad with a large splotch of grime on either cheek, still awaits identification, but concerning the clean, smooth-faced young fellow at the far right—Wiggins, no doubt, for he was taller and older than the rest[13]—there can be no question. In virtually every detail of his person and appearance one immediately observes an unmistakable resemblance to Vincent Starrett, the dean of Sherlockian scholars, as he looked fifty and more years ago. What other prominent latter-day Irregular might have been recognizable in the features of the "street Arab" Charles Doyle omitted from his drawing never will be known.

For his father's artistic ability Conan Doyle had the highest respect. He held the conviction that his parent was an artist "more terrible than Blake."[14] In the faces of the dead Drebber and the "old woman" who called for the ring there are evidences of this awesome graphic power, but as for the portrayals of Sherlock Holmes, there seems to be nothing to do but conclude, sadly and reluctantly, that Charles Doyle knew him not, decidedly not in the flesh, apparently not even so much as in Watson's description of him.

The early fortunes of *A Study in Scarlet* must be traced a little farther. The work attained its next edition late in December, 1891, when Ward, Lock & Bowden brought it out with forty illustrations by George Hutchinson, among which are eleven picturing Holmes. Although none of these comes off quite as effectively as could be desired, they still afford infinitely better delineation of the great man than that previously given him by Friston and Doyle.

Considered solely from the standpoint of historical significance, the most notable of these drawings is the one which shows a smiling, exultant Holmes in the laboratory at the University of London Hospital—where he has just discovered the hemoglobin test for blood stains—advancing toward Watson with a test tube in his hand, unaware that he is about to make the most momentous finding of his entire career: his future Boswell. This portrayal, which is the only early depiction of Holmes at the memorable meeting with Watson, may

have seemed to its maker a perfect reflection of the detective's appearance, yet it falls considerably short of being completely felicitous, probably because it does not emphasize to any noticeable degree that impressive frontal prominence one inevitably associates with a person of the unusual mental development which Holmes is known to have possessed.[15]

Even wider of the mark is a Hutchinsonian representation of Holmes aroused from his apathy at Watson's prodding and hustling into his overcoat preparatory to making a

furious dash by hansom cab to the Brixton Road for the purpose of looking into the bad business at 3, Lauriston Gardens. In this drawing he might well be anyone of his time and years who was tall, angular, and handsome. Another study of the detective, which shows him kneeling by the dead body of the simian-faced Drebber, captures something of the essentiality of the man, but this also is hardly worthy of reproduction. More nearly in character, at least in so far as concerns outward appearances, is a depiction of him as he stands with Gregson and Lestrade looking at the word "Rache," which the artist placed too low on the wall. His features here are very decidedly those of the American Indian type at their heaviest and grimmest, perhaps just a bit too heavy and grim to be truly representative.

They appear again, with greater refinement of expression, in the portrait of Holmes (opposite) with hands on knees, stooped over the dead terrier, which occurs in the illustration that pictures the tense scene in which the test of Hope's pills had just been brought to a successful conclusion. This is by all odds the most lifelike of the portraits done by Hutchinson, who clearly knew Holmes. He had to know him in order to be able to bring out so distinctly a particularity of his appearance concerning which Watson never was too explicit. The doctor's descriptive remarks suggested rather than described it.[16]

Save for a very disappointing full-face sketch of Holmes in seated position scraping at his violin, and for a posterior view of him dogging the "old woman," the remaining illustrations that picture the detective present him with virtually the same features the artist gave him in the drawing which shows him hustling into his overcoat.

*　*　*　*　*　*

While Hutchinson's drawings continued to be used in a number of subsequent printings of *A Study in Scarlet,* it has recently been brought to the attention of Sherlockian bibliographers that he was not the last of the early illustrators of that work.[17] At least one other, James Greig by name, must be added to the list of those who were commissioned to turn their hands to pictorial interpretation of the first Watsonian revelation back in the days when Sherlock Holmes still was fairly young.

The edition for which Greig made his drawings was brought out in 1895 by Ward, Lock & Bowden for presentation with the Christmas number of *The Windsor Magazine.* On its front cover it carried a portrait depicting the artist's conception of Holmes in what undoubtedly was meant to be a contemplative mood, for contemplation is denoted in every aspect of the pose but one—the left eye, unlike the right, is not fixed in abstract, pensive gaze, but has a hard and steely look. Apart from this incongruity, the lean, rugged face with its high forehead, thought-knit brows, and long, thin, beaked nose constitutes a vigorous study in portraiture, which, while not a complete realization of the Holmes of *A Study in Scarlet,* does carry more conviction than either Friston's or Charles Doyle's conceptions. The portrait bears no signature, but there seems to be no reason to doubt that it was the work of the same hand that furnished the illustrations for the text.

Of the seven drawings that Greig did for the text, three depict episodes in which Holmes appeared: his approach to the body of Enoch Drebber, the "old woman's" call at 221B, and the taking of Jefferson Hope there. In none of these is there anyone who bears a strong resemblance to the portrait on the cover, nor are these drawings as clear-cut and forceful as the cover portrait. In fact, Greig's conception of Holmes' looks as displayed in these textual illustrations are very erratic. The Holmes of the first drawing is not readily recognizable in any of the persons depicted in the other two, while the third one really offers a very pretty problem in identification. Hope can be identified easily because of the handcuffs, but which of the other persons portrayed was intended to be Holmes is anybody's guess.

* * * * * *

SHERLOCK HOLMES in

A STUDY IN SCARLET

BY A CONAN·DOYLE

Meanwhile, back in the year prior to the appearance of the first printing of the Hutchinson illustrated edition of *A Study in Scarlet,* further revelation of the doings of Sherlock Holmes had been made by Watson, again under the name and through the agency of his literary go-between, Arthur Conan Doyle, who was to continue to function in that capacity for all of Watson's stories about Holmes.[18] This tale, *The Sign of the Four,* first had publication in America, in the issue of *Lippincott's Magazine* for February, 1890. The only attempt at embellishment of this major piece of the high history of Sherlock Holmes, which offers many dramatic moments for graphic depiction, was a frontispiece picturing an incident in the story told by Jonathan Small that transpired years before the dainty Miss Mary Morstan ever came to Baker Street to consult the detective.

The first book publication of this tale, under the imprint of Spencer Blackett as *The Sign of Four,* London, 1890, also had only a frontispiece, which was done by Charles Kerr. To this artist some measure of thanks is due from the faithful, more for the reason that in his lone drawing he chose to depict an episode of the story in which Holmes had a part than for the aspect he gave the immortal Sherlock.

The scene is the room of the late Bartholomew Sholto at Pondicherry Lodge, with the body of the defunct Bartholomew still upon the premises and Holmes entering upon his investigation of the tragedy while the faithful Watson stands by. Kerr's drawing, says Vincent Starrett in *The Private Life of Sherlock Holmes,* "is a competent but uninspired interpretation of the episode. . . . Just possibly the blot upon our Sherlock's lip is intended to indicate the shade cast by his prodigious nose; it looks, however, like a touch of a moustache. For the rest, there is something statuelike and dauntless in the carriage of the famous head; the legs are statesmanlike in their determined stance; and all in all—what with the somewhat epileptic corpse, and Watson—the picture is a trifle comic."

From our present-day viewpoint the drawing, taken as a whole, admittedly is faintly comic. But if the reader will bear in mind what D. H. Friston and Charles Doyle, who came before Charles Kerr, had made of Sherlock Holmes, he must concede that Kerr's pictorial conception was by far the best one of the detective published up to the year 1890.

SHERLOCK HOLMES in

CHARLES KERR

Meanwhile, too, Dr. Watson had begun to release the series of shorter additions to the canon which ran to twenty-four numbered revelations in *The Strand Magazine* under the general title of "Adventures of Sherlock Holmes."[19] With the appearance of the first tale of this series there entered into the history of the Holmesian portraiture a name destined to remain an enduring part of the cultural heritage of all who were privileged to read these stories as they came out in *The Strand* or in their early English editions. That name was Sidney Paget. Writing of its bearer in his memoirs, Watson's literary go-between called him "poor Sidney Paget," undoubtedly because of his untimely death, and would have it that his brother Walter, also an artist, served as the model for his drawings of Sherlock Holmes.[20] This is clearly conceivable, since Holmes himself was not available for deline-

ation in the flesh, being then somewhere in the mountain fastnesses of Tibet.

For the first twelve stories, later published in book form as *The Adventures of Sherlock Holmes,* Sidney Paget made one hundred and four drawings.[21] Sixty of them picture the great detective. For the second twelve, eleven of which were later published in book form as *The Memoirs of Sherlock Holmes,* this artist did ninety-seven drawings, and again the eminent criminological investigator is portrayed sixty times.[22] An evaluation of every one of these one hundred and twenty drawings in which the master's face and figure appear is uncalled for here. Where so large a number of illustrations is concerned it is inevitable that more than a few of them may be expected to be illustrative merely in a conventional way, with no special claims to detailed attention. Only in connection with a printing of the full text of the stories would there be any justification for reproducing all of them. A selection will have to be made then, to the end that only those shall be considered which picture Holmes most intimately and revealingly, and at the same time exemplify some of the more characteristic methods he employed when at work on his cases.

Those fortunate mortals who purchased the issue of *The Strand Magazine* for July, 1891, and read *A Scandal in Bo-*

SHERLOCK HOLMES in

hemia were introduced in the very first illustration to a tall but not uncommonly spare Holmes standing unconcernedly in profile pose before the fireplace of the Baker Street sitting room and looking the recently married Watson over "in his singular introspective fashion." As he appears (opposite) in a reproduction of Paget's sketch, his chin is somewhat prominent; and his forehead is rather higher than the average, an effect that the artist no doubt found easy to reproduce because of the fact that the hair above Holmes' temples seems to have made a considerable recession by the time he was thirty-four, the age he had attained when he essayed to match his wits against those of *the* woman, Irene Adler. His cheekbones, too, are high, but his nose, though long and fairly large, has none of that beakiness which would suggest the Red Indian.

Indeed, from this initial portrait in *The Strand* the beholder receives the impression that Holmes was a much better-looking figure of a man than Watson would have his readers believe, an impression that some of the later drawings for these twenty-four stories also convey. By way of further example, consider Holmes as he is shown receiving Miss Mary Sutherland in *A Case of Identity,* easily the one representation

of all the one hundred and twenty that pictures him at his handsomest. And there are other drawings which could be cited that portray him looking only a shade less elegant in person and appearance than a popular matinee idol. But not all of the portraits are after this pattern. Many of them, the greater number of them in fact, present a detective whose features, though striking in appearance, are not quite so cloyingly handsome. These form a series for which a certain well-known personator of Holmes on the stage, the screen, and the radio could have served as the model if he had been available in the early nineties. As for the rest of the illustrations which provide presentments of Holmes, these sometimes come very close to delineating the man Watson portrayed in his word-picture. Here the detective's looks often verge on ugliness, and at times a more than shadowy suggestion of the Amerind type is perceptible. The exceedingly good-looking Holmes of the aforementioned illustration for *A Case of Identity,* the Holmes who, as Watson stated in *A Scandal in Bohemia,* "never spoke of the softer passions, save with a gibe and a sneer," has only to be compared with the downright unhandsome Holmes of *The Naval Treaty* exclaiming, "What a lovely thing a rose is!" in order to perceive how great a range of dissimilarity there was in the portraits made of him for this series of adventures.

It has been asserted that this extreme variance in the artist's depictions of his subject did not come about intentionally, but was caused by the crude execution of some of the engravings made to reproduce the original drawings. The explanation might prove acceptable if all the engravings had been produced by one man whose execution was inclined to be variable. But from first to last, at least six different engravers are known to have been employed in reproducing Paget's illustrations for *The Adventures* and *The Memoirs,* each one of whom made his blocks after his own style and consequently left the mark of his own technique upon them. Under the circumstances, a noticeable lack of uniformity in the Holmesian portraiture was inevitable.

All six engravers had a hand in making the various cuts for the illustrations of *The Adventures,* but only one of them appears to have had anything to do with the making of those for *The Memoirs.*[23] By far the greater number of the blocks for the first eleven stories of *The Adventures* are signed "W

& S," or a variation of these initials, apparently designating two men who, between them, did nearly all of the signed engravings for *A Scandal in Bohemia*, *A Case of Identity*, *The Man with the Twisted Lip*, and *The Boscombe Valley Mystery*, and all of the signed reproductions of the illustrations for *The Red-Headed League*, *The Five Orange Pips*, *The Blue Carbuncle*, *The Speckled Band*, *The Engineer's Thumb*, *The Noble Bachelor*, and *The Beryl Coronet*. Another engraver who reproduced all the Paget drawings for *The Copper Beeches*, and whose work bears a close resemblance to that of the foregoing, is identified only by the initials "AR" with "Co" just below. The unknown engravers associated with these initials were the ones who invariably made Holmes very easy on the eye, altogether too easy in many instances.

A few excellent illustrations for *A Case of Identity* and *The Boscombe Valley Mystery* were from engravings signed "J. Swain, Sc.," and the best one of the reproductions of Paget's drawings for *The Man with the Twisted Lip* (and for the entire series of *The Adventures*, and *The Memoirs* too) bears the signature "Hare, Sc."[24] Swain's Holmes is very angular and has a weathered, hard-bitten look which contrasts markedly with the more regular-featured and generally sleek-appearing detective in the engravings signed "W. & S." Had Swain given Holmes a beaky nose, his reproductions of Paget's portraiture would have come very close to matching Watson's description of the man. Hare's superb engraving for *The Man with the Twisted Lip* shows more aquilinity than any of the other reproductions of Paget's drawings of Holmes, and it is this feature that undoubtedly contributes much toward making the portrait seem greatly superior to all the others in *The Adventures* and *The Memoirs*. In the Holmes of Hare's engraving is mirrored the sort of detective most clients expected to meet when they called at 221B, that is, a personality radiating strength and mental power, and not a yawning, listless-looking fellow, who so often came far short of their conceptions of how a famous consultant in crime should look and act.

One man responsible for the engraving of several minor illustrations for *A Scandal in Bohemia* signed himself "P. Naumann" in one of his cuts for that story, and it was he who reproduced all of Paget's drawings for *The Memoirs*.

At least, all those that are signed bear the initials "P. N." The Holmes of his engravings is variable in mien and runs the gamut from the very good-looking to the very unhandsome. Naumann is the only one of the six against whom a case could be made on the grounds of crude execution of engravings. But strangely enough, the portraiture of Holmes in his less carefully executed work comes nearest to meeting Watson's description of the detective.

Of course, the inveterate Sherlockophile will want to know which engraver reproduced Paget's conception of Holmes most faithfully, but to satisfy anyone's curiosity on that point without recourse to the original drawings, all of which may or may not now be available, is out of the question. And speculation on the subject would seem to be inadvisable, since it could very easily lead to acrimonious and possibly schismatic controversy. Unquestioning acceptance of all the portraits may be too much to ask. The best that can be hoped for is that the student, having made his personal selections, will not summarily reject the rest.

In his first drawing of Holmes, Paget presented the detective in a frock coat, and appropriately too, for a visitor was expected, a very distinguished one as events proved. And frock-coated Paget's illustrations generally show Holmes when he was at home in Baker Street, though oftener than not, and particularly at those times when there were no cases on hand to harness the power of his racing, impatient brain, he wore a dressing gown. Reading the agony columns of *The Times,* or sawing away at his violin into the small hours of the morning, or busy with scissors and paste keeping his scrapbooks up to date, or lounging about reading his black-letter editions, he seems to have preferred this piece of apparel. He even wore it sometimes when he did chemical investigations; Paget pictures him (opposite) garbed thus at the experiment on which he was working when Watson brought him the problem of *The Naval Treaty,* one of only half a dozen or so of the drawings for *The Adventures* and *The Memoirs* that show him in his dressing gown.

There were other kinds of attire, of course, both for home wear and for going out. Watson makes mention more than once of Holmes as being tweed-suited. And for travel there was a long, gray cloak and a close-fitting cloth cap. Clothes, it is said, do not make the man; yet in Holmes' case the attire, whether donned for comfort, for travel, or for the purposes of detection, was not wholly incidental. What he wore did contribute in some degree toward making him the greatly loved detective that he then was, and, for that matter, still is. But regardless of the sort of raiment with which Paget clothed his subject, the artist's drawings are to be prized much more highly for the glimpses they provide of the detective's mannerisms and methods than for any indication they may be of the nature and extent of his wardrobe.

The student need not seek very far among the illustrations for *A Scandal in Bohemia* before he encounters a drawing that represents the great man in one of his characteristic attitudes (overleaf). It is at that point in the tale where Holmes, ready to hear his haughty client's story and impatient at his slowness in getting around to it, has remarked that if his Majesty would condescend to state his case it would be easier to advise him. The picturization is excellent, even though it is more or less rear-view. There is another, later drawing of Holmes in the same pose that presents him in pro-

file view: the illustration which pictures him listening to the
story of Miss Violet Hunter, who had had an unusually attrac-
tive offer to go as governess at the Copper Beeches, five
miles beyond Winchester. He is comfortably settled in his
armchair, fingertips together and elbows resting on the arms
of the chair. It is a pose that he was to repeat many, many
times during his long and active career, the pose he was wont
to assume while his clients unburdened themselves of their

woes and their problems. Watson, who often described it,
called this his "judicial mood."[25] Sometimes Holmes varied
the posture slightly, as when he placed his elbows on his knees,
which necessitated his leaning forward, in which position he
must have presented a less judicial aspect.

Once his client's problem was known, Holmes suited his
methods to the requirements of the case. In the one which
Miss Hunter brought to his attention it was a matter of waiting for developments. A large number of his cases called for
more immediate action, which usually entailed a hurried jour-
ney to the scene of the crime, if crime it was that had been
committed. But when the puzzler happened to be one like that
with which Jabez Wilson, erstwhile member of the Red-Headed
League, confronted Holmes, a preliminary period of mental
digestion was in order. For this process the great fathomer
also had a special pose: he sat "curled . . . up in his chair,
with his thin knees drawn up to his hawk-like nose, . . . with
his eyes closed and his black clay pipe thrusting out like the
bill of some strange bird."[26] Paget did not capture this pose
too faithfully (above). Holmes seems to have relaxed into a
more comfortable position than Watson's description of the
detective's looks as he mulled over the singular business involving the red-headed pawnbroker of Coburg Square would indicate. This singular business was "quite a three pipe problem,"
Holmes informed Watson, begging the doctor not to speak
to him for fifty minutes.

It does not require the mention of pipes to remind the
dyed-in-the-wool devotee that Holmes was addicted to the
use of tobacco to about the same extent to which he had become habituated to the processes of ratiocination. Nearly always there was a thick haze of pungent blue smoke contributing
considerably to a lowering of the visibility in the Baker Street
sitting room whenever Holmes was on the premises, and this

haze continued to become denser and denser as more and more smoke billowed upward in puffs from his pipe, or cigar, or cigarette, until the atmosphere inside often was much foggier than it ever became outside in Baker Street. The reader knows that this is not an exaggeration: he has Watson's word for it.[27] (See page 54.)

Paget seems to have considered the cigarette taboo for illustrative purposes. In these drawings, too, he never pictures Holmes smoking a cigar, though Watson infrequently appears with one. Mostly with Holmes it was the black clay pipe, old and oily, which, Watson tells us, "was to him as a counsellor."[28] Through the aid of its inspiriting fumes he solved many a knotty problem. Occasionally, "when he was in a disputatious rather than a meditative mood," he would lay aside the clay and take up the long-stemmed cherry-wood pipe which he is seen lighting with a glowing cinder, picked from the hearth with a pair of tongs, in the first illustration for *The Copper Beeches,* while he rather pointedly criticizes Watson's methods of chronicling his cases.

For country use he appears to have preferred an old and time-tried briar, less fragile than the clay and presumably easier to pocket. He had this briar with him at Lee, in Kent, when, sitting cross-legged in his blue dressing gown upon a pile of cushions and pillows, he smoked the whole night through over the problem of the disappearance of Mr. Neville St. Clair and consumed an ounce of shag tobacco in the process. Paget has a picture of him as Watson saw him there upon awaking in the morning, the pipe still between his lips, the

SHERLOCK HOLMES in

smoke still curling upward, but nothing left on the floor where the pile of shag had been when the doctor retired. This was not an unusual accomplishment for a man who was wont to smoke for his before-breakfast bracer a pipe "composed of all the plugs and dottles of the day before," which he had first placed carefully on a corner of the mantelpiece to dry.[29]

Holmes' concern with tobacco was not limited solely to his inveterate and abandoned use of it; he knew the weed thoroughly in all its forms and byproducts. By sight or by smell alone he could identify any cigar that was ever made. A whiff of the tobacco in the lone cigar left in Blessington's cigarcase was enough to tell him that it was a Havana; and a look at the cigar ends tossed into the fireplace of the resident patient's room by the other members of the Worthington bank gang enabled him to identify them as of the peculiar kind of cigars imported by the Dutch from their East Indian possessions. He had even made a special study of tobacco ashes; had, in fact, written a monograph on the subject, *Upon the Distinction between the Ashes of the Various Tobaccos,* in which he enumerated "a hundred and forty forms of cigar, cigarette, and pipe tobacco," and provided "coloured plates illustrating the difference in the ash."[30]

He was an authority on all sorts of pipes also, and could deduce much from them concerning the attributes, habits, and character of their owners. "Pipes [he once said] are occasionally of extraordinary interest. Nothing has more individu-

ality, save perhaps watches and boot-laces."[31] He held Mr. Grant Munro's amber-stemmed old briar in his hand when he spoke these words, and his duly ordained delineator sketched him thus.

Paget rarely failed to portray Holmes in whatever make-up he chose to put on in those instances when the exigencies of a case required him to do some on-the-spot investigations in the assumed appearance and personality of someone not at all likely to be taken for a detective. The artist pictured him in both of the disguises he used while working on *A Scandal in Bohemia*: the first as a drunken-looking groom, "ill-kempt and side-whiskered, with an inflamed face and disreputable clothes," in which get-up he was pressed into service as a witness to the marriage of *the* woman Irene Adler, spinster, to Godfrey Norton, Esq., at the Church of St. Monica in the Edgeware Road on March 23, 1888; the second, on the same day, as "an amiable and simple-minded Nonconformist clergyman" (on page opposite) who, by a ruse adapted from M. Dupin's bag of tricks, intended to make Irene reveal where she kept the photograph in which she had posed with the King of Bohemia. Paget also drew Holmes "dressed as a common loafer," in which guise he had gone out and solved the theft of the beryl coronet. "With his collar turned up, his shiny, seedy coat, his red cravat, and his worn boots he was [says Watson] a perfect sample of the class." The artist has also shown him (top of page 28) as an old man, "very thin, very wrinkled, bent with age," the disguise he assumed one night in June, 1889, when he was seeking a clue to the supposed murder of Mr. Neville St. Clair at the Bar of Gold in Upper Swandam Lane. For editorial reasons, perhaps, the

SHERLOCK HOLMES in

opium pipe which Watson states was a part of his disguise did not get into the picture. But infinitely better than all these delineations is Paget's fine portrait of Holmes in what undoubtedly was his most masterly piece of deception occurring in this series of stories. It appears in *The Final Problem,* where the detective found it necessary to assume the habit and manner of an aged Italian priest (overleaf, at foot of page) in order to avoid the attentions of Professor Moriarty, which had become altogether too pressing for Holmes' personal safety on the morning of April 25, 1891.

His adeptness at make-up certainly was beyond criticism. He took in Athelney Jones of Scotland Yard at least once; and on five different occasions he is known to have taken in his closest associate, who said of him that in putting on disguise "it was not merely that Holmes changed his costume. His expression, his manner, his very soul seemed to vary with every fresh part that he assumed."[32] That he must have had to maintain a very extensive wardrobe for such purposes is evident, for his biographer has stated that at one time "he had at least five small refuges in different parts of London, in which he was able to change his personality."[33]

Not only was Holmes able to pass himself off successfully in any *rôle* he chose to assume; he could also feign sudden seizures, such as cataleptic fits, and other forms of illness, with such appearance of naturalness as to deceive all onlookers, including the medically trained Watson. It suffices for present purposes to adduce but one instance, the incident in the case of the Reigate murder when Holmes' face "suddenly assumed the most dreadful expression. His eyes rolled upward, his features writhed in agony, and with a suppressed groan he dropped on his face upon the ground." Such art in simulation presupposes an early period of some years on the stage. Holmes himself never spoke of any Thespian apprenticeship on his part, which is not surprising, for he was unusually close-mouthed about the years of his youth, but Dr. Watson, who has many references to his propensity for histrionics and his susceptibility to admiration and applause, undoubtedly had knowledge of some such phase in Holmes' early life. How else would one reconcile the circumstances with the doctor's statement that "the stage lost a fine actor . . . when he became a specialist in crime?"[34] If he had known that Holmes never acted on the stage, is it not much more likely that the doctor,

who had a neat sense of the niceties of diction, would have said, "the stage failed to gain a fine actor?"

It would seem that when Holmes attended the theatre it was neither the drama nor musical comedy that drew him there. Performances of instrumental music and the opera were his preferences and in them he took the utmost delight, a fact that need not cause any wonder when one remembers that he himself was no mean performer on the violin, and a composer of some note besides. Paget presents him in one such attendance at the theatre, St. James' Hall it was, where he sat all afternoon in the stalls, "gently waving his long, thin fingers in time to the music," another Holmes altogether, with dreamy, languid eyes and smiling face, completely enraptured by the music that Sarasate made on the violin.

To Holmes doubtless belongs much of the credit for giving to the detecting fraternity its traditional occupational badge, the deerstalker cap, which he sometimes wore, with a long, gray traveling cloak, when his cases required him to go out of the city. But Paget comes in for his rightful share of the credit too, since he helped to confirm the fore-and-after as detection's authenticating trademark, at least for stage, story, and picture, by depicting Holmes in it whenever Watson described him as being so covered in these adventures. Though Holmes' earliest pictorial presentation to the public in a deerstalker occurred in the first illustration for *The Boscombe Valley Mystery,* which engaged his attention in June, 1889,

SHERLOCK HOLMES in

he is known to have affected this sort of headgear as early as 1881, a fact of which Paget took cognizance when he did the drawings for *Silver Blaze*. Here, again in the first illustration, Holmes, *en route* with Watson by train to King's Pyland in Dartmoor to look into the supposed murder of John Straker and the disappearance of the horse Silver Blaze, is shown wearing his ear-flapped traveling cap.

Among the illustrations for *The Boscombe Valley Mystery* is one which presents Holmes in the most unusual portrait Paget ever did of him. It pictures the detective in the horizontal, almost literally trying to sniff out clues. As the artist depicts him here on the trail of Charles McCarthy's murderer, he actually has a houndlike appearance, but the limitations of Paget's medium prevented him from reflecting in his drawing all that Dr. Watson attempted to convey in his description of the detective as he looked at such times.

"Sherlock Holmes [says Watson] was transformed when he was hot upon . . . a scent. His face flushed and darkened. His brows were drawn into two hard lines, while his eyes shone out from beneath them with a steely glitter. His face was bent forward, his shoulders bowed, his lips compressed, and the veins stood out like whipcord in his long, sinewy neck. His nostrils seemed to dilate with a purely animal lust for the chase, and his mind was so absolutely concentrated upon the matter before him that a question or remark fell unheeded upon his ears, or, at the most, only provoked a quick, impatient snarl in reply."[35] Holmes' manner and appearance when he struck a warm trail while asearch for clues were previously described in lesser detail in *A Study in Scarlet*[36] and *The Sign of the Four*.[37] This drawing of Paget's was the first attempt by any artist to represent them pictorially.

Three of the stories in the series known as *The Memoirs* will always hold a special fascination for the faithful because of what they reveal concerning the origins, the family, and the early years of Sherlock Holmes. These stories are *The Gloria Scott, The Musgrave Ritual,* and *The Greek Interpreter*. While the information they contain upon these several subjects is much too meager, to find fault with them on that score is of no avail: besides some little additional light that Paget's illustrations shed, there is nothing more of a factual nature to be learned concerning those subjects from any other printed sources.

It was in *The Greek Interpreter* that Watson, after nine years' association with Holmes, first learned that the detective had a brother, who was seven years his senior and possessed keener powers of observation and deduction than he did, but lacked the ambition and the energy to apply them for effective and successful criminological investigation. Mycroft Holmes, who moved in a very circumscribed orbit, was always to be found at the Diogenes Club of an evening, between the hours of quarter to five and twenty to eight, and Sherlock took Watson around there to meet the man who sometimes was the British government. Assumably, Paget also was a member of the club, and on hand that evening to sketch a portrait of the corpulent Mycroft which may rightfully be hung in the Holmesian gallery. It portrays him as he looked at the age of forty-three. (Illustration at left.)

SHERLOCK HOLMES in

Watson learned something too upon that memorable evening concerning the ancestry of the Holmes brothers. One of their grandmothers was a sister of Horace Vernet, the renowned French artist,[38] and from her Sherlock was inclined to believe that he had inherited his genius. "Art in the blood [he said] is liable to take the strangest forms." His kinship with the Vernets has a deep and as yet unplumbed significance for another reason. Holmes said nothing to Watson about it—at least, no mention of it occurs in the Writings—but it seems to be a well-substantiated fact that at the middle of the last century there was another Horace Vernet, also an artist, and presumably a cousin to Sherlock, who lived in Charleston, South Carolina, where he followed his profession and instructed others in it,[39] and where, some researcher in the lives and doings of the Vernets and their descendants doubtless will find, Sherlock spent some of the years of his youth and so had his first experience of America and acquired the groundwork of his wide acquaintance with American ways, the evidences of which have been so thoroughly documented by Christopher Morley in "Was Sherlock Holmes an American?"

On the strength of other equally significant passages in the canon it may be assumed that young Sherlock also spent some time in France visiting with his Vernet relatives there. And since his great-uncle Horace lived until 1863, in which year Sherlock became nine, it is well within the bounds of possibility that the great artist may have done a portrait of his sister's precocious grandson before putting off mortality for immortality.

The Gloria Scott, Sherlock's first case at twenty-one, is pure Holmesian incunabulum: Watson never recorded anything of Holmes' life prior to the events of this story. From it are to be had some few facts about his college days and an account of the circumstances that first caused him seriously to consider making scientific detection his lifework. Naturally, one proceeds to an examination of the illustrations Paget did for this story with a tingle of quickening interest, for here young Sherlock is portrayed as he looked on the threshold of his majority. Of the several drawings in which he appears, the best is the one picturing him seated in a garden chair upon the lawn of the Trevor country place at Donnithorpe in Norfolk, where he was spending "a month of the long vacation" with

his college friend Victor Trevor. According to Paget, the eye-arresting combination of features which distinguished the Holmes whom Watson described in *A Study in Scarlet* already was very strongly marked, so strongly, in fact, that there could be no mistaking the identity of the young man as he sits there, cross-legged, in the garden chair. The thin, elongated nose, the determined thrust of the chin, the observant and penetrating eyes, so deep-set that they almost look like holes in the long and narrow head that is the natural complement to a form as tall and lean as his was, preclude any guesswork. This definitely is Sherlock Holmes, *aetat.* xxi. The portrait presents him dressed for summer comfort: white shoes, white suit, white straw hat, the only dark touches being his hat band, his tie, and his socks. The Trevors wear bowlers and are otherwise more formally and heavily attired.

The Musgrave Ritual, Sherlock's third case, is the source of what little additional information has been made available concerning his undergraduate life, his preparations for his profession, and the first years of his practice. Unfortunately, the illustrations that Paget drew for the story contribute nothing of any importance to early Holmesian portraiture, and therefore none of them merits reproduction on that score. What is of greatest interest pictorially is a drawing showing Holmes at the large tin box which he had hauled out from his bedroom one winter night of indeterminate date upon Watson's insistence that the sitting room be tidied up. In this box he kept all the records of his early cases. There were, as he

SHERLOCK HOLMES in

put it, "some pretty little problems among them"—the record of the Tarleton murders, the case of Vamberry, the wine merchant, the adventure of the old Russian woman, the singular affair of the aluminum crutch, the full account of Ricoletti of the club foot and his abominable wife, the reminders of the adventure of the Musgrave Ritual; and save for the account of this last, that is all the record that Watson ever left of them. He isn't any more informative on the question as to whether the accumulation of papers in the sitting room was or was not put in order that night after Holmes had finished his narrative of the facts concerned with the lost crown of the Stuarts and its discovery at Hurlstone Manor.

In Holmes' profession, violence was bound to be an almost daily experience: an engineer barely escapes death by hydraulic pressure but loses a thumb; an elderly man in a seedy, battered billycock becomes involved with a mob of ruffians and in attempting to defend himself breaks a window and loses his Christmas goose; one of the promoters of the Franco-Midland Hardware Company reads in *The Evening Standard* of the failure of an attempt upon Mawson and Williams, stockbrokers in Lombard Street, London, and almost succeeds in committing suicide in the hardware company's "temporary" offices at 126B Corporation Street, Birmingham; the Reigate squires make a murderous assault upon Holmes when he is broken in health and not physically able to defend himself.

The list could readily be extended to several pages without including a single instance of death by violence, which also was a commonplace to Holmes. And of course he sometimes had to resort to violent action himself when his quarry, run

to earth, made show of resistance. His physique was by no means a true indication of his actual strength. Tall and lean though he was, he nevertheless had muscles of steel and was capable of furious and powerful action when the need for it arose. Paget did sketches of him in a number of those situations where he showed uncommon outbursts of physical activity. As the artist pictured him lashing with his cane at the deadly speckled band, he is the veritable personification of superhuman energy unleashed. Incidentally, by driving the viper back upon its master, he contributed in some part to the death of Dr. Grimesby Roylott, a fact which apparently caused him no disturbance of conscience and, consequently, no loss of sleep.

His interview with Sir George Burnwell, in the case of the beryl coronet theft, did not come to an exchange of blows. Quick thinking and prompt action, however, were called for, and Holmes proved equal to the occasion. Clapping a pistol to Sir George's head resolved the matter thoroughly and convincingly, although one may question whether Holmes' method of clapping a pistol, as illustrated by Paget, was the proper one to employ in so far as the safety of the clapper was concerned.

The Stockbroker's Clerk and *A Case of Identity* each contain a picture of Holmes in fast and furious action, but since in both instances the artist's interpretation deviated somewhat from the textual content, the drawings are not reproduced here. Neither of these incidents involved any actual physical combat.

The most celebrated of Holmes' jousts was his mighty clash with Professor Moriarty, "the Napoleon of crime," as the detective so aptly described this brilliant but criminally inclined mathematical genius, who was for years the behind-

SHERLOCK HOLMES in

the-scenes machinator of half that was evil and of nearly all that went undetected in the criminal annals of London. From the time that Holmes first became aware of the existence of this latter-day Jonathan Wild and resolved to rid the world of him, it was inevitable that some day their paths would cross. They did cross, apparently for the first time, on the morning of April 24, 1891, when the door of the sitting room at 221B Baker Street opened and Holmes looked up to see Moriarty standing upon the threshold.

Paget's portrait of the Professor confirms Holmes' description of him. He was tall, thin, and round-shouldered, with an exceptionally high-domed forehead, from beneath which his relentless eyes, deep-set in a long forbidding face, glared forth in a manner boding no good to the detective, who observed that his head was "forever oscillating from side to side in a curiously reptilian fashion." Moriarty's object in calling at 221B was to prevail upon Holmes to desist from incommoding him in the pursuit of his nefarious activities. When Holmes stood fast, the professor gave utterance to some highly minatory remarks and took his departure, inexorably committed to the removal of the detective from the world of the living.

The showdown, as all Sherlockians know, came not in London, but at the falls of the Reichenbach in Switzerland, where Paget depicts them locked in mortal combat upon the very brink of the fearful, yawning chasm. Holmes' deerstalker has become dislodged and is to be seen falling into space. Since the drawing is captioned "The Death of Sherlock Holmes," the only inference the artist left to be drawn was that the owner of the deerstalker shortly followed it into the abyss. Paget does not show that as actually having happened, and Watson was not there to see. In any case, Holmes had disappeared when the doctor returned from the wild goose chase upon which Moriarty had drawn him. "An examination by experts," Watson later wrote, left "little doubt that a personal contest between the two men ended, as it could hardly fail to end in such a situation, in their reeling over, locked in each other's arms." Thus, Watson concluded, did "the best and the wisest man" he had ever known go to his death. How unsound were the conclusions he drew regarding the outcome of the affair he learned only about three months after the publication of *The Final Problem*.[40]

SHERLOCK HOLMES in

Sherlock Holmes did occasionally take Watson to task for the manner of his presentations of the adventures, but he never seems to have had any fault to find with Paget's illustrative work. As a matter of fact, this artist had done very handsomely, sometimes too handsomely, by him. Had he been so minded, he could have found sufficient cause for dissatisfaction on the score of verisimilitude alone, but since he probably felt flattered by Paget's treatment of his form and figure, he remained silent upon the subject. One cannot help wondering, however, what his reactions were to the efforts of his early American portrayers.

The full story of the printing and illustration of the *Adventures* in American newspapers, if it is ever written, should prove to be the strangest chapter in the history of the emission of the canon. S. S. McClure, in his *Autobiography*, claims the credit for having distributed the series to the newspapers subscribing to his syndicate, and, while nothing occurs anywhere in connection with the stories so far found printed in the newspapers that may be construed as corroboration of his claim, no adequate reason for doubting his statement has yet been advanced.

Thus far, one or more of the *Adventures* have been found in *The Baltimore Weekly Sun, The Boston Daily Traveler, The Buffalo Courier, The Chicago Inter Ocean, The Cincinnati Times-Star, The Louisville Courier-Journal, The New Orleans Daily Picayune, The Philadelphia Inquirer, The Philadelphia Press, The Toledo Daily Blade, The Toledo Weekly Blade,* and *The Washington Post,* on various dates between July 11, 1891, and June 19, 1892. Further search undoubtedly will bring other purveyors of the stories to light, with some printings of a date later than the one last mentioned.

The Baltimore Weekly Sun and *The Boston Daily Traveler* were not subscribers to the syndicate service. *The Sun* reprinted the first three *Adventures* at dates subsequent to those of their initial American appearances, with credits to *The Strand Magazine* for *A Scandal in Bohemia,* which title was transformed into *Woman's Wit,* and *A Case of Identity,* and to *The Louisville Courier-Journal* for *The Red-Headed League,* with its title reduced to *Red-Headed League. The Daily Traveler* reprinted *The Red-Headed League* two weeks after its very earliest release in any other newspaper without giving credit to any person or publication. *The Toledo Weekly*

Blade reprinted *A Scandal in Bohemia* and *The Red-Headed League* from *The Daily Blade* exactly as each one had appeared in the latter newspaper seventeen days earlier. None of these papers printed the entire series of the *Adventures*. *The Courier-Journal* heads the list with ten, *Inter Ocean* printed nine, *The Inquirer*, six, *The Courier* and *The Times-Star*, four each, but not the same four, *The Daily Blade*, three, *The Post*, two, and *The Daily Picayune*, only one.

The first story of the *Adventures*, as released to the syndicate's subscribers, was printed between the dates of July 11 and July 15, 1891, under several variations of its original title. In *Inter Ocean* and *The Courier-Journal* on July 11, *The Courier* and *The Post* on July 12, and *The Times-Star* on July 14 and 15 it had for its title *A Scandal of Bohemia*, in *The Daily Blade* on July 13 it was *Scandal of Bohemia*, and in *The Daily Picayune* on July 12, *A Bohemian Scandal*. The dates, of course, are the chief index to the syndicate subscribers. Then, too, in all the newspapers of these dates except *The Post*, the name of A. Conan Doyle, or sometimes merely Conan Doyle, is followed by the words, "author of *Micah Clarke, The White Company*, etc.," and in the case of *The Post* the similarity of the illustrations further determines that newspaper's inclusion in the list of subscribers. The syndicate provided two illustrations for the embellishment of the story, which had to be redrawn by the art staffs of the several newspapers that reproduced them, and it would seem that the story could be purchased without the illustrations. In any case, their use was not mandatory, for only the *Inter Ocean, Daily Picayune, Daily Blade*, and *Post* appearances of the story were accompanied by the drawings, which, in their redrawn states, did not turn out uniformly.[41]

McClure relates that when he syndicated *The Black Arrow*, by Robert Louis Stevenson, he provided his subscribers with illustrations for the story done by Will Low, a well-known artist whose work commanded a sizable monetary return. He seems to have gone to no such trouble and expense for *A Scandal in Bohemia*. Here is no great-name artist. In fact, here is no name at all, only anonymity. When one considers the drawings, the absence of identification is quite understandable. The first illustration (not shown), a small one of Holmes at the moment when the King of Bohemia removes his mask, has no special quality to recommend it. Holmes is

SHERLOCK HOLMES in

merely an undistinguished representation of the figure of a
male human being. The second drawing presents the detective lying on the couch in the sitting room at Briony Lodge,
dressed in what the artist supposed to be the guise of "an
amiable and simple-minded Nonconformist clergyman." And
Holmes, as he is portrayed here, might well be taken for a
cleric, not so much because of his garb as for the cast of his
countenance. The drawing may then be considered an excellent portrait of the detective in disguise, but of "Shelley
plain" there is no actual, intimate glimpse, for, as Watson
said on the occasion, "his expression, his manner, his very
soul seemed to vary with every fresh part that he assumed."

Portrait and Profile

With the release of *The Red-Headed League,* the erratic practices of the syndicate and its subscribers with regard to the distribution and printing of the Watsonian revelations begin to become even more noticeable. McClure seems to have provided no illustrations for the story, and of the seven papers named above, the only ones to print it about the scheduled time of its release were *Inter Ocean* and *The Courier-Journal,* on August 8, and *The Daily Blade,* on August 10. *The Philadelphia Press,* a new addition to the list of subscribers, printed the story on August 9. Two of these, *Inter Ocean* and *The Press,* carried illustrations, the first paper one, the other four. The *Inter Ocean* drawing, a portrait signed "C.," undoubtedly was a product of the imagination of one of the artists on its staff. Although the presence of the aureole could very well cause the observer to assume that the red-headed pawnbroker of Saxe-Coburg Square is portrayed here, even one who has had no experience of pawnbrokers would be hard put to accept as representative of their calling a person wearing a monocle. No, this is not the obese and nondescriptly dressed Jabez Wilson, and that leaves only Sherlock Holmes, whom the artist probably depicted thus without reading the story. The handlebar mustache and the monocle we have become accustomed to associate with a certain type of Victorian Englishman, among them being the retired colonels of the Indian Army. In fact, the subject could very plausibly be Colonel Sebastian Moran, but he, at this time, had not yet made his obnoxious presence felt in the canon.

The illustrations in *The Press* printing of *The Red-Headed League,* undoubtedly drawn by a staff artist especially for the occasion, are not signed. This circumstance need not be a cause for regret, since no great unknown portrayer of the master detective will remain unsung because of the anonymity of his work. And yet there would be some small satisfaction in knowing the artist's identity for another reason. While his portrayals of Holmes are indifferently done, one of the drawings is as fine a represent of the outward aspects of a small corner of the London milieu circa 1890 as will be found among all the illustrations ever made for the embellishment of the canon. It catches the very spirit of the time and place. The figures of Holmes and Watson, the hansom cab, the gas light, all are in perfect keeping with the aura that hung over Saxe-Coburg Square, where Jabez Wilson

had his pawnbroker's shop, and over Baker Street, too, in those far-off days when the problem of the duped red-head engaged the attention of the great fathomer. The drawing deserves to be rescued from the moldering pages of *The Press*.

In so far as the portraiture of Holmes is concerned, it has been seen that the illustrators of the first two stories failed to comprehend their subject. The same is likewise true of the illustrators of the other *Adventures* that have been found in American newspapers, of the printing and illustration of which some brief account will be given, without further example of the latter. *A Case of Identity*, in *Inter Ocean* on September 5 and *The Post* on September 6, had three illustrations in each case; those in the former were signed "B.," those in the latter were initialed "C. K. B." In *The Daily Blade*, on

September 7, there were only two illustrations. *The Courier-Journal* printed the story on September 5, and *The Times-Star* on September 8 and 9, both without illustrations.

If drawings were supplied by the syndicate for *The Boscombe Valley Mystery,* printed in *Inter Ocean* and *The Courier-Journal* on October 17, in *The Courier* on October 18, and in *The Times-Star* on October 20, 21, and 22, none of these newspapers saw fit to use them.

The next story, titled *The Adventures of the Orange Pips* in *The Courier* on November 8, had no illustrations; as *Adventures of Five Orange Pips* it appeared in *Inter Ocean* on November 7, with two drawings signed "B.," and in *The Courier-Journal* on the same date with one illustration, the first one used for any of the stories so far printed by this newspaper.

The same newspapers printed the next story in the series as *The Man with a Twisted Lip. The Courier* printed it on December 6, without illustrations, *The Courier-Journal* on December 5, and *Inter Ocean* on December 6—the last two newspapers with three drawings signed "B.," a syndicate artist, and probably the same "B." or "C. K. B." of *A Case of Identity* and *Adventures of Five Orange Pips.* In addition to these newspapers, *The Philadelphia Inquirer* appears for the first time as a syndicate subscriber with its printing of the story on December 6 under the title, *The Strange Tale of a Beggar,* with two drawings also signed "B."

The Adventure of the Blue Carbuncle was found in *The Courier-Journal* of January 9, 1892, without illustrations, and, as *The Christmas Goose that Swallowed the Diamond,* in *The Inquirer* of January 10, with two illustrations by R. C. Swayze, the first of these newspaper artists so far identified by his full name. Until further illustrated printings of the story are found, it is not possible to determine whether Swayze was in the pay of the syndicate or of *The Inquirer.*

The Speckled Band has been found only in *The Inquirer,* where it was printed on February 14, with one illustration signed "F. C. Drake," the second definite identification among these inept portrayers of the master detective.

The Engineer's Thumb has not been located in any newspaper and probably was not distributed by the syndicate. In any case, *The Noble Bachelor* appeared in America more than three weeks in advance of its publication in *The Strand*

Magazine. Under that title it was printed in *Inter Ocean* on March 13, where there were two illustrations signed by Drake. As *The Adventure of the Noble Bachelor,* the story appeared in *The Courier-Journal* on March 12, with one illustration signed "F. C. Drake." *The Inquirer,* on March 13, entitled it *The Story of the Missing Bride* and used one illustration, signed "Drake."

The Beryl Coronet appeared in *Inter Ocean* on April 17 and 24, with three illustrations; as *The Adventure of the Beryl Coronet,* its original *Strand* title, it was printed in *The Courier-Journal* on April 17 and 24, with no illustrations, and in *The Inquirer* on the same dates with one drawing, signed "Drake."

The final story of the *Adventures* was printed as *The Copper Beeches* by *Inter Ocean* on June 12 and 19, using four illustrations signed "W. B.," and as *The Adventure of the Copper Beeches* by *The Courier-Journal* on June 11 and 18, with one drawing, also signed "W. B." *The Inquirer* likewise printed the story, on June 12 and 19, under the second title, with four illustrations, three of which were signed "W. B.," who was a syndicate artist.

It will have been noted that, from the time of the printing of *The Red-Headed League,* the newspapers followed no set scheme for use of the drawings. In few instances do the same illustrations appear throughout for even one story. It would seem that possibly as many as five or six drawings were supplied by the syndicate artists, from which the several newspapers made such selections as pleased them. Of the newspapers mentioned, only two of those which printed the first *Adventure* were in at the final story, namely *Inter Ocean* and *The Courier-Journal.* *The Inquirer,* which began its printings of the stories with *The Man with the Twisted Lip,* or as there entitled, *The Strange Tale of a Beggar,* was also in at the end.

After their run in the newspapers, the stories were published by Harper & Brothers in 1892 as *The Adventures of Sherlock Holmes,* with sixteen of the original Paget drawings. America, so far, had contributed nothing of exceptional note to the portraiture of Sherlock Holmes.

The second dozen of the stories made much more interesting history in the rather erratic course of their American magazine and book publications. *The Cardboard Box,* the first of this series to appear here, was printed in *Harper's Weekly* for January 14, 1893, without illustrations. Next, in the same periodical, came *The Yellow Face,* then *Silver Blaze,* and thereafter all the rest except *The Final Problem,* in their original order, with illustrations to the number of twenty-one by W. H. Hyde, an artist of undeniable ability, but one almost utterly unqualified for doing any portraiture of the world's most famous consulting detective. He was handicapped from the beginning by the very serious disadvantage of having neither personal acquaintance with Sherlock Holmes nor the least inkling of the nature of his appearance. This becomes all too painfully evident from his initial illustration, for *The Yellow Face,* which presents his conception of Holmes examining Mr. Grant Munro's amber-stemmed pipe. The possession of the

SHERLOCK HOLMES in

most superficial knowledge of the canon as it stood revealed up to that time would have restrained Hyde from picturing a Holmes so handsome and regular of feature, with such pretty cupid's-bow lips. It would also have prevented him from presenting a Holmes so impeccably turned out in narrow-brimmed, high-crowned bowler and short, light overcoat, with—shall one say?—accessories to match. This is not Holmes the incisive reasoner, the quietly prim detective of Baker Street that appears here; this is a dilettante, the best dressed man about town. Hyde might at least have spared Watson's readers the hat: Holmes was not in the habit of wearing it in his rooms.

It is true that all the other illustrators so far did, either through ignorance or intent, take some liberties with the person and appearance of Sherlock Holmes as described by Watson. Even Paget, the best of them, had strayed. But in his case the liberties were more than offset by the excellence of his drawings, and therefore his sins could be condoned. At its best, the result of Paget's efforts always was recognizable as a portrait of Holmes. The same cannot be said of Hyde's performance. And he seems to have realized that his conception of Holmes was far from what it should have been: in all his twenty-one illustrations he attempted only five depictions of the detective, and among these there is little or no similarity of feature.

By one of those strange turns of fortune that are to be met with sometimes in publishing history, *The Final Problem* did not bring the second series of stories to a close in *Harper's Weekly,* but made its first American appearance in *McClure's Magazine,* thereby escaping illustration by Hyde and coming to be embellished with eleven admirable drawings executed by Harry C. Edwards. Of the eight which picture Holmes only one is more than exceptionally good, and that one is a masterpiece of Holmesian portraiture. It shows the detective as Watson saw him at the moment of turning away to go back to the Englischer Hof at Meiringen in response to what he assumed was the landlord's request that he come and administer to a dying Englishwoman. Watson began to think some hours later, and continued to be certain for some years to come, that it was the last glimpse he would ever have of Holmes. Never did he expect to see his friend again in this world.

Alpenstock at his side, Holmes stands at the end of the path with his back against a rock and his arms folded, gravely contemplating the raging ferment of waters below, in complete readiness for the expected advent of Professor Moriarty. He wears his deerstalker and it tends to accentuate that strongly marked aquilinity of feature which Edwards reproduced so faithfully and so well. Holmes may appear a little more stockily built than one would suppose him to have been from Watson's description, yet the portrait is from every point of view a more satisfactory one than any Paget had done in his illustrations for *The Adventures* and *The Memoirs*. Seeing him depicted so ably here in what purportedly was the final chapter of his career, more than a few of his American admirers must have regretted that Harry C. Edwards had not had the opportunity to illustrate all of the twenty-four stories in the series.

Harper & Brothers' first printing of the second series in book form contained all twelve of the stories, and twenty-seven illustrations, five of them by Paget, twenty-two by Hyde, the latter having furnished an additional drawing for *The Stockbroker's Clerk,* which did not contain a portrait of Holmes. Paget's illustrations were divided between *The Cardboard Box* and *The Final Problem,* three for the former and

SHERLOCK HOLMES in

two for the latter. When objections were raised, presumably by Watson, to the inclusion of *The Cardboard Box* in the American edition, Harpers issued a second printing from which that story was omitted. But the strangest part about the publication of *The Memoirs* here was that none of Edwards' drawings for *The Final Problem* got into the book. Thus, the finest pictorial interpretation of the great fathomer that had been produced for the adornment of the canon up to this time was left buried in the back files of a popular magazine and gradually became lost to the memory of all but a few of his most devoted admirers. It is true that it was to be far surpassed in the years to come by the work of the greatest of all portraitists of Sherlock Holmes, yet it has deserved a better fate than that which has been its lot.

* * * * * *

All Sherlockophiles know that on May 6, 1891, the *Journal de Genève,* in what probably was a very limited number of last-run copies, carried a startling and saddening piece of news: an account of the death of Sherlock Holmes in the chasm of the Reichenbach falls. But whether the *Journal* of that date also contained a photograph of the great detective they cannot say, since that is a question which probably will not be resolved until someone turns up one of the copies in which the account was printed. Actually, it is a matter of no great moment, for the portraiture of Holmes that accompanied the publications of Dr. Watson's earlier revelations had provided many fine likenesses. The numerous works of Sidney Paget attained the highest standard of excellence among the English illustrators, while the American artist Harry C. Edwards, in one of the several drawings he did for the illustration of *The Final Problem* when it was published about two years after the Reichenbach incident, achieved the most satisfying portrait of the detective made up to that time.

Happily for Holmes, and for all those who take delight in everything pertaining to him, the account in the *Journal de Genève* for May 6, 1891, proved to be "grossly exaggerated," as Mark Twain is said to have remarked upon hearing a premature report of his own death. The great detective was destined to live and to work for many more

years, and to be limned again and again, not only by Sidney
Paget, but, best of all, by the American artist Frederic Dorr
Steele. However, once Paget's drawings for *The Hound of
the Baskervilles* and for *The Return of Sherlock Holmes*
have been considered, these notes will treat mainly of Steele's
magnificent delineations, while only passing notice will be
taken of the work of the later English artists because of
copyright coverage.

The Final Problem, well-documented as it is by references
to the account of the affair at the falls of the Reichenbach
printed in the *Journal de Genève* of May 6, 1891, to Reuter's
dispatch in the English papers on May 7, and to the letters
of Colonel Moriarty, printed in the public press in an attempt on his part to defend the memory of his late brother,
would seem to have left the followers of Sherlock Holmes
every reason to believe that their hero was dead. To all
appearances they were free to bestow their allegiance elsewhere, but instead of doing so, they continued to hold the
assurance all the while that somehow there must have been
a mistake, that their Sherlock was not really dead. In that
assurance they stood fully as confident as did Mycroft Holmes
and Colonel Sebastian Moran in their knowledge that Holmes
had not died in the falls of the Reichenbach. Dr. Watson
became startlingly aware of that fact too, early in April
of the year 1894, but his hand was stayed by Sherlock's
strict injunction against any disclosure of what had really
happened. At the same time Scotland Yard was let into the
secret. But a secret it could not remain for long. After
Holmes resumed his practice and his presence gradually came
to be felt by the criminal elements, rumors began to get about
concerning his return and the great successes he was attaining
in his work. And then, his name was once more in the newspapers.[42]

At that there undoubtedly was the greatest rejoicing
among the faithful. But though they continued to take up each
new number of *The Strand Magazine,* as they had unfailingly
done throughout the months and the years since the account
of his death was published there, in the expectation that they
would be vouchsafed some further word of Holmes and his
remarkable doings, still no new revelations were forthcoming.
Even their long-held hope that Watson would continue to
enlarge the canon from the notes he had of the many un-

recorded cases did not materialize. Now that it was a certainty that Holmes was back in harness, and still no tales of new adventures had come from the hand of his biographer, it would not have been at all surprising if the faithful had given themselves over to dolorous outcry, making "How long, O Watson, how long?" the burden of their lament.

At long last, however, their watchfulness had its reward. It was in August, 1901, that Watson began to unfold the hair-raising business of *The Hound of the Baskervilles* in *The Strand Magazine,* where it ran through nine consecutive numbers. By the unknowing this tale of Holmes and the horrendous hound could hardly fail to be accepted as posthumous revelation, since the incidents related therein took place some time before his supposed demise, with no intimation whatsoever given as to whether he still was among the living or lying in the abyss of the Reichenbach.

The elect knew better, of course, and to them this further emission of Holmesian lore from the inspired Watson's hand would have been altogether beatific in itself. But their cup of happiness did not merely run to the full; it brimmed over, for there were illustrations too, and while some of them left much to be desired in the way of Holmesian portraiture, their shortcomings were offset to some extent by the fact that they were done by none other than the well-beloved and long-remembered Sidney Paget. He made sixty drawings for the embellishment of *The Hound of the Baskervilles,* in thirty-two of which the face and figure of the master appear. Among them are some very effective profiles, and also some inexcusably inept depictions. But the veteran readers of *The Strand Magazine* probably did not mind. They had their beloved Sherlock back again, and in their joy at having him back it is unlikely that they had any thought of being captious about Paget's portraiture; it must be supposed that they were minded rather to exclaim to themselves with a deep inner contentment, as Holmes once exclaimed to Watson, "This is, indeed, like the old days."

The Hound gets under way, as many of the adventures do, with one of those typically Holmesian demonstrations of the science of deduction that the detective delighted to stage, and Paget proceeds forthwith to picture Holmes, the same familiar Holmes whom he had sketched so often of old, examining with his convex lens the object proemial, which in this instance was the Penang lawyer left behind in the Baker Street sitting room by a caller who had found no one at home at 221B. By the time Dr. James Mortimer returned to Baker Street, Holmes had pretty well exhausted the possibilities of the cane as a source of light on the life and characteristics of its owner. Of course he could not deduce from it that this amiable, absentminded, and unambitious country physician was so fervid a connoisseur of skulls that he would admire his to the point of coveting it; nor that he would bring with him a problem that, the detective came to have no doubt, was just about the most complex "of all the five hundred cases of capital importance" he had handled up to that time.

The account of the origin of the hellish hound which Hugo Baskerville had set down in 1742, for the enlightenment and admonition of his sons, Holmes pooh-poohed as so much folklore. But Dr. Mortimer's recital of the circumstances attendant upon Sir Charles Baskerville's death, concluding with the dramatic disclosure that he had found "the footprints of a gigantic hound" near the place where Sir Charles came to his end, was of a more immediate and more tangible fabric which could not be brushed aside so easily. Nor could Holmes disregard the succession of incidents pointing to the machinations of a coldly calculating sinister force directed at the personal safety of Sir Henry Baskerville that had begun to make itself evident almost from the moment of the new baronet's arrival in London. As a matter of fact, Holmes soon realized that he had indeed found a "foeman" worthy of his steel. Paget made a pictorial representation showing Holmes at the moment when he first spotted this foeman as he was spying, from behind false whiskers, upon Sir Henry in Regent Street. In his faultless frock coat and his immaculate topper he looks very much more like a cabinet minister or distinguished diplomat with urgent business awaiting him at Number 10 Downing Street than like a detective on the trail of a man who, eventually, was found to have a dog that very definitely did something in the nighttime.[43]

With his leavetaking of Sir Henry Baskerville, Dr. Watson, and Dr. Mortimer at Paddington on their departure for the baronet's ancestral hall in Devonshire, Holmes recedes for a time from the center of the stage. Paget chose his reentry into the spotlight to do a long-range view of him, as the mysterious man whom Watson saw upon the moor on the

SHERLOCK HOLMES in

night he and Sir Henry sallied forth in an attempt to take
Selden, the Notting Hill murderer. His subject stood upon
the jagged pinnacle of the Black Tor, "outlined as black as
an ebony statue" for a long moment against the background
of the low moon's silver disc, and then he was gone. His
figure, Watson says, was that "of a tall, thin man. He stood
with his legs a little separated, his arms folded, his head
bowed, as if he were brooding over that enormous wilderness
of peat and granite which lay before him. He might have
been the very spirit of that terrible place."

And Watson, had he not been so overwrought at the
moment, might then have guessed the identity of this "tall,
thin man." But as he did not, and as his curiosity had been
so deeply aroused, he grimly set himself the task of stalking
this mysterious moor dweller to his abiding place. When he
found the rude neolithic hut with its signs of recent habitation,
there shortly ensued another of those highly dramatic moments

in which the tale abounds. And Paget pictured it, showing the shadow that "fell across the opening of the hut" as "in cold, incisive, ironical voice" the approaching unknown said, "It is a lovely evening, my dear Watson." But any devotee who has the canon indelibly fixed in his memory will suspect that the silhouette which lies across the doorway of the hut is not exactly what it should be. Paget made an inexcusable slip here, the nature of which becomes fully apparent in the next illustration (not reproduced here), in which Holmes, seated

SIDNEY PAGET

SHERLOCK HOLMES in

upon a stone ouside the hut, does not wear his cloth cap, as Watson so unequivocally states he did, but his head is covered with a battered, disreputable-looking affair that may be a cloth hat.

How did this glaring discrepancy between context and illustration come about? It is difficult to assign the exact reason, but the likeliest explanation would seem to be that Paget, because of other considerations, had fallen into error through an inattentive reading of Watson's text. In any case, this lapse, which is repeated in all the Holmesian portraits that follow, weakened his delineative conceptions very noticeably.

Holmes has his biographer by his side again, the somber story moves on to its spine-chilling climax, and Paget provides further illustrations. Two of them picture the hound magnificently, but add nothing of any significance to Holmesian portraiture. One of them is that in which Holmes is shown as he gets his first glimpse of the hound; the other, that in which the hound is pictured at the end of its diabolical career upon the moor. Holmes knew, of course, that it was a material hound he had set out to run to earth, but not even his strong nerves were proof against the horrifying thing that burst out of the fog enveloping Merripit House and came bounding along on the trail of Sir Henry Baskerville. Watson states that at sight of it Holmes' eyes, which had been "shining brightly in the moonlight" just a moment before, "started forward in a rigid, fixed stare, and his lips parted in amazement." Watson himself was too paralyzed to act, and Lestrade let out a yell of terror and threw himself face downward on the ground. In his depiction of the scene Paget left no cause for anyone to wonder why this should have been so, and why the hound got by Holmes and Watson before they had so far recovered themselves as to be able to make use of their weapons. Their shots proved ineffective then, and the hound loped on. Only when it had already seized Sir Henry by the throat did Holmes again come within safe firing distance. Paget's drawing pictures him as he was discharging five barrels of his revolver into the flank of the devilishly disguised animal, thus dissipating forever the myth of the infernal hound that had plagued the house of Baskerville for so many years.

The English book publication of *The Hound of the Baskervilles,* by George Newnes in 1902, contained only sixteen

SHERLOCK HOLMES *in*

of the original sixty Paget drawings. In the United States the story was first published in the American edition of *The Strand Magazine*,[44] with all of Paget's drawings. Thereafter it was given book form under the imprint of McClure, Phillips & Company, with eight of the original *Strand* illustrations, six of which had not been used in the Newnes edition.

* * * * * *

An American artist made further contributions to the gallery of Holmesian portraiture when, about the time the McClure, Phillips edition came into the book shops, *The Hound* was secured for serialization by *The Courier-Journal* of Louisville, Kentucky. The story began to run in the pages of its Sunday edition on July 6, 1902, and the first ten weekly installments were accompanied by illustrations.[45] Four of these were Paget originals, the remaining six were new drawings by Robert M. Hoof, who provided several depicting scenes the English artist had not delineated. Holmes appears in three of Hoof's drawings. The first one is a quarter-length portrait of the detective, showing him with a large round head and a broad forehead, from which the hair has begun to recede. His chin is long, as is his nose, though the latter is not noticeably beaked. Holmes looks quite prim in an exceedingly high stiff collar that cannot have been anything but a hindrance to free and easy ratiocination.

Hoof did much better by Holmes in a second drawing, which portrays the detective as Watson found him upon returning to 221B after spending the day at his club. The good doctor's first impression, as he tells us, was that a fire had broken out in the rooms, for so dense was the smoke that the light of the lamp on the table was dimmed by it. But, as Watson soon observed, there was no fire, there was only Holmes surrounded by the results of his being lost in tobacco and the problem of the strange hound that prowled the moors of Devonshire, and Hoof delineated the scene quite realistically. (Opposite page.)

Hoof's third drawing of Holmes presents him at long range as the mysterious man whom Watson saw upon the moor the night Sir Henry and he sallied forth in an attempt to take Selden, the Notting Hill murderer. Paget had delineated the same scene to somewhat better effect. (Page 51.)

* * * * * *

The actual outcome of the encounter between Holmes and Moriarty at the falls of the Reichenbach upon that memorable day of May 4, 1891, was finally revealed for all to read in *The Empty House,* the first of the series of thirteen stories that began in *The Strand Magazine* for October, 1903, and ran to December, 1904, the adventures known in their book publications as *The Return of Sherlock Holmes.* Twelve of them are accounts of cases that engaged Holmes' attention between the years 1894 and 1901, when he reputedly was at the height of his powers; one, the case involving the odious Charles Augustus Milverton, goes back to the middle eighties.

That these tales were pseudorevelation, and their protagonist an imposter, as some have presumed to aver, is sheer delusion, for their authenticity is fully substantiated by the illustrations, which are by Sidney Paget. Had this not been the real Holmes who had returned, Paget surely would have been able to detect the fraud and expose it; he would not

SHERLOCK HOLMES in

knowingly have lent his talents to the perpetration of any such deception upon the master's followers.

The drawings for *The Return* run to ninety-five, and there are presentments of Holmes in eighty-one of them. It is not to be expected that among so many depictions every one should be a masterpiece of portraiture and therefore warrant individual notice. The fact of the matter is that few of them rise above the high level which Paget attained in that section of the Holmesian gallery which already houses the previously considered portraits of the detective he did for *The Adventures* and *The Memoirs*. At least two which picture Holmes in dramatic situation and mirror some characteristic attribute of his are so outstanding as to make them especially desirable additions to that collection.

One of them occurs among the drawings which Paget provided for *The Solitary Cyclist*. It depicts Holmes in fine fistic form, poking a straight left at the villainly Woodley, after having failed to avoid completely a vicious backhander just delivered by the aforesaid Woodley. A very pleasing companion piece to this drawing would be a portrait in natural colors showing Holmes as he looked upon his return to Baker Street that evening, with a cut on his lip, a large discolored lump on his forehead, and his usually neat appearance so disordered that Watson says he "wore a general air of dissipation which would have made his own person the fitting subject of a Scotland Yard investigation." The incident did not discompose Holmes inwardly. On the contrary, he was vastly amused by it all. This was not the only occasion upon which he had come home bearing signs of adverse conflict: there was, to mention only one instance, the time one Mathews knocked out his left canine in the waiting room at Charing Cross.

Another depiction for which the confirmed Sherlockophile should be everlastingly grateful is the first illustration Paget executed for *The Abbey Grange*. In the opening paragraphs of this story there is recounted one of the most memorable episodes in the long association of the detective and his biographer, and the depiction Paget did of it must be given special consideration in any canvass of the Holmesian drawings that might be undertaken for the purpose of selecting the perfect frontispiece to an illustrated edition of the canon. It shows Holmes as he arouses the slumbering Watson "on a bitterly

cold and frosty morning, towards the end of the winter of
'97," with his stirring view-halloo to evil-doers, "Come, Watson, come! The game is afoot!" Other Holmesian utterances
there may be which are more widely known and more fre-
quently quoted, but of all Sherlock's sayings the most cherished
in the hearts of his devotees assuredly is "Come, Watson,
come! The game is afoot!" The words have an urgency about
them as compelling as that of the opening lines of the Rever-
end John Walter's famous evangelistic hymn:

"Kommt, brüder, kommt, wir eilen fort
Nach neu Jerusalem."

Of course it was not to *the* New Jerusalem that Holmes,
with candle in hand, was calling Watson, but for the good
doctor the words were, even "on a bitterly cold and frosty
morning," an irresistible summons to the nearest earthly
approximation to a New Jerusalem that he could have desired.
Upon hearing them, he stood ready for any adventure, willing
to risk any danger by the side of his friend. Only the words
of deep concern that Holmes spoke upon the several occasions
when the doctor suffered injury while assisting the master
huntsman in the apprehension of desperate criminals could
possibly have moved him more. "Come, Watson, come!"
always will bring a thrill to someone's heart as long as the
name of Sherlock Holmes continues to be revered.

These two drawings must be counted among the finest
that Paget made of Sherlock Holmes. As for the over-all
impression that one gathers from a consideration of all the
portraits appearing in this collection of stories, one senses
that Holmes' bearing has become more masterful, his presence

more imperious and commanding. A more pronounced beakiness of countenance may have contributed somewhat toward imparting this effect, which is particularly noticeable in those delineations that present him in his deerstalker; and Paget, by reason of some happy inspiration, has covered him with this distinctive piece of headgear in one or more of the illustrations for at least half of the adventures of *The Return*.

Whatever new quality has become manifest in Sidney Paget's portraiture since he drew the illustrations for *The Hound of the Baskervilles*, it seems quite certain that it is not attributable to any impression that may have been made upon the artist by William Gillette's masterly interpretations of the Holmesian ego in his play, *Sherlock Holmes*, which was presented at the Lyceum Theatre in London during the winter of 1901-1902, following a two-season run in New York. Tall and slender in figure, aquiline in feature, self-contained and forceful in stage presence, Gillette was eminently fitted by physical make-up and histrionic gifts to personate the real Holmes with astonishing fidelity. One critic hailed his work in the *rôle* as "the almost perfect personification" of the immortal detective,[46] an act of judgment with which no one would presume to take issue. This same critic, however, having scored one bull's-eye, let go with a second shot from his critical blunderbuss and missed the target altogether: he also professed to see in Gillette complete embodiment of the Holmes of Paget's drawings! At the time expression was given to this conviction it would have been impossible to make out a well-grounded brief in its support. So far, the only Holmesian portraits in which a really close resemblance to Gillette could be detected were to be found in the fine drawings of Harry C. Edwards for *The Final Problem*, and their publication, strange to remark, took place some six years before William Gillette ever played Sherlock Holmes. Paget's portraiture at no time reflected any quality which would indicate that he had been influenced by Gillette's performance in *Sherlock Holmes*.

After the concluding story of the series that comprises *The Return* had had publication in *The Strand Magazine*, it was fated that there would be no more pictures of the detective signed with the initials "S. P.," for Sidney Paget died in 1908, before release of further revelations took place. To those who had followed his work in *The Strand* from the time *A*

Scandal in Bohemia appeared there his passing came as a deep personal loss. His portraits had become for millions of his countrymen everywhere the accepted imagery of the great fathomer. So strong indeed was the influence of Paget's work in his own land that its mark is on the drawings of all the English illustrators of Watson's revelations who came after him, and many examples of their Holmesian portraiture could very easily be mistaken for the product of his hand if they were not identified in their *Strand* appearances by names other than his.

In the English book publication of *The Return of Sherlock Holmes,* by George Newnes in 1905, only sixteen of the original ninety-five drawings that Paget made to accompany the printings of the stories in *The Strand Magazine* were used.

* * * * * *

The same series of stories that contained the last, and the best, of the Holmes drawings by the greatest of the English illustrators of the canon also served as the vehicle for the advent among Holmesian portraitists of the American artist Frederic Dorr Steele, whose picturizations of the detective were to attain a much greater renown than Paget's, although the English artist's drawings always were highly competent.

For the text of the stories of *The Return,* which made its first American appearances in various numbers of *Collier's Weekly* from September 26, 1903, to January 28, 1905, Steele drew forty-six illustrations. The master detective's visage appears in twenty-six of them. For each story Steele also provided individual headpieces and decorative initials. But at the most these drawings, though of very special merit, comprise the lesser part of this artist's contribution to the embellishment of *The Return.* The choicest of his drawings for this section of the canon consist of the ten gorgeous portraits which he executed in color for the front covers of a like number of the issues of *Collier's* in which Watson's stories appeared. These portraits were the finest of Holmes done up to that time, perhaps the finest that ever were or ever will be done of him.

Frederic Dorr Steele probably never knew Sherlock Holmes in the everyday sense of human acquaintanceship, and he may never actually have set foot in Baker Street in all his days. Nevertheless, his drawings reveal a truer conception of his subject than any that is reflected in the works of his predecessors who were privileged to record first-hand impressions. Steele clearly had been a student of the canon and an admirer of Holmes before he received his commission to illustrate the stories of *The Return*. As he was to remark some thirty years later, he found it "odd that the 'great hawk's bill of a nose' so explicitly described . . . [by Watson] was ignored by the English draughtsmen for so many years," and he proceeded at once to portray Holmes with a very conspicuously aquiline cast of countenance. He had not then seen Gillette play Sherlock Holmes and, according to his own recollection, did not see him in the *rôle* until some months after his drawings for *The Return* had been completed, yet in retrospect he could write: "I did not need to be told to make . . . Sherlock Holmes look like Gillette. The thing was inevitable. I kept him in mind and even copied or adapted parts of a few of the stage photographs."[47]

It would seem to have been inevitable too, though the eventuality could not possibly have been foreseen by Steele at the time, that the resulting image would come to be accepted as the most satisfying of all. And for a very good reason: Steele was completely in accord with the Holmesian personality from the beginning. His portrait of the great huntsman on the cover of the issue of *Collier's* in which *The Empty House* appeared set a standard in Holmesian portraiture that Steele himself did not always meet and only rarely overtopped afterwards. This, of all the cover portraits, is at once the least like any of the stage photographs of Gillette and the most nearly like Holmes as Watson had described him. (See page 62.) It has no identifying caption, nor does it need one. That kneeling figure, anyone who has ever read *The Empty House* will tell you, is Sherlock Holmes on the brink of the Reichenbach chasm, watching his archenemy Moriarty fall to his death. There is no trace of elation on the tense, angular features that are as rigidly set as if they had been carved in stone. They still display all the grim determination that Holmes felt about the necessity of ridding the world of an evil genius. Indeed, it is doubtful whether he ever exulted in his victory over Moriarty. His expression conveys the feeling that the necessity for the Professor's removal from the world of the living had not been of his choosing, that it had been an unpleasant piece of business which the Professor had forced

upon him, and that the nature of its conclusion left him more
than a little sad. The student of the canon will have noted
that the subject of Moriarty's end was one upon which he did
not care to dwell at any length; the account he gave Watson
contains only the barest details concerning the affair.

Although all of Steele's drawings appearing in connection
with the text of *The Empty House* are excellent, only the
decorative detail of the initial letter will be reproduced here.
It is a true-to-life silhouette of the master himself upon the
drawn shade which brought a gasp and a cry of amazement
from Watson as he glimpsed it from across the way in Cam-
den House. The deep and sharply outlined shadow on the

SHERLOCK HOLMES in

shade was cast by the bust in wax which had been moulded from life for Holmes by Monsieur Oscar Meunier of Grenoble just prior to the detective's return to London. Before that night's work was done, Colonel Sebastian Moran had put a large, gaping hole in the bust with a projectile shot from his airgun; "plumb in the middle of the back of the head and smack through the brain" was the way Holmes described the feat. The bust presumably was damaged beyond all possibility of restoration to its original condition. In any case, no record exists of its display in any of the places where waxworks have been exhibited, and therefore it seems safe to assume that because of the effects of the expanding bullet from the Colonel's airgun there was lost to the world an iconographic masterpiece the value of which would now be incalculable.

Steele's next cover portrait, for the issue of *Collier's* containing *The Norwood Builder,* presented again in large-size form his famed profile of Holmes' finely proportioned head in all its craglike aquilinity. The episode pictured would seem to be that in which Holmes studies what Watson described as "the well-marked print of a thumb" on the wall in the hall of the wily Jonas Oldacre's house. But the print is a handprint, and Holmes did not wear his dressing gown to Lower Norwood. Steele himself has admitted that the print had nothing to do with Hector McFarlane's thumb, or even with *The Norwood Builder*, and that it was put in merely to suggest what one might expect to see upon the walls of Holmes' rooms at 221B Baker Street.[48] The portrait was the first one drawn from a photograph of William Gillette. (See page 64.)

In the cover portrait for the issue of *Collier's* that contained *The Solitary Cyclist* Holmes is pictured at home in Baker Street "as he pulled at his meditative pipe" and speculated upon the whys and wherefores of the mystifying experiences Miss Violet Smith had met with upon the lonely road that runs from Chiltern Grange to Farnham and passes between Charlington Heath and Charlington Hall. It would seem that, in his estimation, the case was not a three-pipe problem like that of *The Red-Headed League,* for he proceeded to pack Watson off to Surrey to play detective. The portrait evidently is a very close adaptation of one of the stage photographs of Gillette. An intimate glimpse of the atmosphere of the sitting room at 221B is afforded in that

part of the background detail which shows Holmes' index volumes of the lives of the criminally inclined ranged upon the book shelves.

The only full frontal view of Holmes in this series of large-size portraits was done for the cover of the issue of *Collier's* in which the story called *The Adventure of the Priory School* appeared. He is shown in the Peak Country here. (See page 66.) In the background is the grove of trees known as the Ragged Shaw, beyond which the roof and chimneys of Dr. Thornycroft Huxtable's select Priory School are visible.

SHERLOCK HOLMES in

This portrait is, of the entire series, the one most nearly like Gillette and seems to be an almost exact copy of a stage photograph of the actor that was first published in *William Gillette in Sherlock Holmes,* the illustrated souvenir program of the Garrick Theatre staging of the drama, which bears the imprint of R. H. Russell, New York, 1900. The same photograph is to be found reproduced in the first edition of Vincent Starrett's *Private Life of Sherlock Holmes.*

Portrait and Profile

The portrait of Holmes on the cover of the issue of *Collier's* that contained *The Adventure of Black Peter* is another choice addition to the celebrated profiles of the detective that Steele patently took a great deal of pleasure in doing. (Page opposite.) That they were done so well when the element of time undoubtedly was not always adequate should be evidence enough of the great care and interest he bestowed upon his work; and that the art editor of *Collier's* may have had to remind him on more than one occasion that his illustrations were due before he could lavish upon them all the affection he felt for his subject may easily be surmised from a very revealing bit of Steeleana related by Ellery Queen in *The Misadventures of Sherlock Holmes*:

"Shortly before *The Misadventures* went to press (about a year or so before F. D. S.'s death), your Editors purchased an original drawing of Sherlock Holmes from Mr. Steele, . . . a large blue-white-and-black drawing of Holmes and Watson examining the dead body of Selden under the 'cold, clear moon' of the Devonshire Moor. This superb piece of work

was done in 1939 for Twentieth Century-Fox, to advertise the motion-picture version of *The Hound of the Baskervilles,* starring Basil Rathbone and Nigel Bruce.

"When the drawing arrived, your Editors drank it in. Then we noticed a queer thing about it: the deerstalkered head of Sherlock was drawn on an irregular piece of board *pasted into* the larger board. Scenting a mystery (*The Adventure of the Second Head*), we asked Mr. Steele if he remembered any tidbit of history connected with that paste-in.

" 'No,' he said; 'Nothing at all interesting.'

" 'You simply didn't like the first head you drew,' we said, 'and replaced it with a second one before sending the drawing to Twentieth Century-Fox?'

" ' Oh, no,' Mr. Steele replied. 'I drew that new head only a week ago—just before sending it to you.'

"It took a few moments for Mr. Steele's soft-spoken and almost casual reply to sink in. Then we grasped the full implications. Long after the drawing had been finished, years after it had served its commercial purpose, four years in fact after it had been bought and paid for by Twentieth Century-Fox, Mr. Steele was still working on it, still improving it—and for no other reason than the sheer love of his subject."[49]

For the cover of the number of *Collier's* in which the case of Charles Augustus Milverton was recounted Steele made a drawing that has to do with the story of this loathsome blackmailer, but it portrays the greatly daring noble lady who "did him in," and Holmes himself is not in evidence. The text of this story has but one illustration picturing the detective, and he is shown in his disguise as a rising young plumber, his pockets loaded down with tools. While Steele supplied a portrait here that Paget omitted to provide, he did not go far enough. Sherlockians would have been delighted with a drawing showing "the rising young plumber" walking out with Agatha, Milverton's housemaid, to whom he had become "engaged." It is not likely, though, that he carried his plumbing tools with him on those occasions as he is shown doing here. To have done so would undoubtedly have been overplaying the *rôle.*

In the tousle-haired, sternly inquisitorial Holmes that was drawn for the cover of the issue of *Collier's* containing *The Three Students* Steele made a very striking side view so utterly unlike his other profile portraits of the detective that

SHERLOCK HOLMES in

"The Adventure of the Three Students"

Collier's
Household Number for November

THE
ADVENTURE
of the
GOLDEN
PINCE-NEZ

SHERLOCK HOLMES in

it comes as a surprising and altogether pleasing variation. The scene, as the books and the student lamp on the desk reveal, is the study of Mr. Hilton Soames, the tutor and lecturer at the College of St. Luke's who prevailed upon Holmes to put aside the researches he was doing in early English charters and look into the mystery of the examination paper in Greek that had been tampered with. It is not so easy to identify the particular incident Steele intended the drawing to picture, though it seems very likely that he meant it to be a portrait of Holmes as he was conducting his second interrogation of Soames' servant, Bannister.

The profile portrait of Holmes from the cover of the issue of *Collier's* in which *The Golden Pince-Nez* was printed is after the more familiar pattern that Steele had by then made famous. Although the pince-nez Holmes holds before his eyes were not his own, it is evident that he could have worn them with distinction if they had been of the proper size for his long, thin nose and narrow face. They had been brought to him in Baker Street from Yoxley Old Place by Inspector Stanley Hopkins, and provided valuable clues leading to the clarification of the strange circumstances attendant upon the death of Mr. Willoughby Smith, secretary to Professor Sergius Coram, who had in preparation an analysis of the documents found in the Coptic monasteries of Syria and Egypt, work upon which the fateful arrival of the professor's wife caused to be suspended for a time.

The drawing of Holmes with Jeremy Dixon's white-and-tan Pompey on the leash, which appeared on the cover of the issue of *Collier's* containing the next Watsonian revelation, namely, *The Missing Three-Quarter,* is highly reminiscent of Steele's first large-size portrait of the detective. He wears much the same sort of attire in both, but a more important point of similarity is the same grim expression of inexorable purpose on his face. (See next page.) He actually has the appearance of being much more houndlike than Pompey, and much more intent upon tracking his quarry down, though it really was the draghound's nose, and not any unusual application of Holmes' extraordinary powers, that led to the finding, under the most tragic circumstances, of Godfrey Staunton, the missing Cambridge University athlete, whose whereabouts Dr. Leslie Armstrong had tried so hard to conceal.

A Holmes in a mood of a very different sort is portrayed on the cover of the issue of *Collier's* containing *The Abbey Grange*. The look on his face is not that of the tensely eager huntsman, the alert and minutely thorough searcher for clues. It is almost casual, almost that of a disinterested observer. His expression, as he undertakes examination of the heavy oaken chair in which Lady Brackenstall had been bound and the crimson cord, with its frayed end, that had been used to

THE ADVENTURE
of the
MISSING THREE-QUARTER

SHERLOCK HOLMES in

THE ADVENTURE *of the* ABBEY GRANGE

secure her, betrays not even the slightest sign of what little puzzlement he did feel regarding that lady's account of the circumstances under which her husband came to his death. So far as Holmes appears to have been concerned at the moment, the case was closed and he was ready to leave. He did leave, but he returned shortly to prove Lady Brackenstall's story an elaborate fabrication.

The issue of *Collier's* containing *The Second Stain,* the story that Watson, for reasons which he stated in its opening paragraph, then thought to be the last Holmesian revelation he would ever give to the public, bore on its cover a portrait that caught Holmes in a pose quite unlike any of those in the large-size picturizations Steele had previously done of him. The detective is in a stooping position before a screen, holding in his left hand a corner of the square of carpet that lay in the front room of the house at 16 Godolphin Street, and

SHERLOCK HOLMES i

examining the great crimson splotch made on it by the blood of the late Mr. Eduardo Lucas, international agent. The drawing undoubtedly was meant to portray Holmes at the very moment when he deduced that the change made in the position of the carpet, by a person or persons unknown to Lestrade, indicated the presence of a hiding place in the floor beneath it.

* * * * * *

Although *Collier's* enlistment of the talents of Frederic Dorr Steele for the pictorial interpretation of the Watsonian revelations contained in *The Return of Sherlock Holmes* had brought about one of those rare marriages of text and illustration that turn out extraordinarily well, the happy and harmonious state of this union seems to have escaped the eye of the art director of McClure, Phillips and Company, the publishing firm which issued the stories in book form in America. Instead of availing itself of the finest run of drawings that had yet been made for the embellishment of any of the Holmesian adventures, this firm commissioned one Charles Raymond Macauley, a newspaper cartoonist, to do thirteen new drawings, one to illustrate each story.[50] Among these drawings there are five containing depictions of the detective. These several portraits reveal a towering raw-boned figure in ill-fitting clothes. Two or three of them emphasize a beakiness of nose and a determined, outward-jutting chin to such an extent that Holmes appears downright ugly. The artist's conception of Sherlock, in close-up, bears a perceptible resemblance to William Gillette. The portraiture also reflects some traces of the Steele influence, and while greatly superior to the efforts of the earliest delineators of the detective, it does not come off too favorably when compared with Harry C. Edwards' fine work, with Paget at his best, or with the scintillating drawings of Frederic Dorr Steele.

* * * * * *

The publication of *The Second Stain* in *Collier's* was accompanied by an announcement to the effect that the story was the last that Watson would ever write about Sherlock Holmes. It appears that it was not through any choice on Watson's part that the revelations were to come to an end: Sherlock Holmes had merely resolved that there should be no more relations of his experiences in detection and he made his decision known to Watson in so peremptory a manner that the latter could hardly fail to respect the wishes of his old friend. The reason advanced by Holmes for objecting to the continued publication of his adventures was that it would serve to draw undue attention to him at a time when he desired to avoid all notoriety. The fact of the matter was that he had abandoned active practice and was living in retirement on the Sussex Downs with the intention of spending the rest of his days in the keeping of bees and the study of philosophy.

As regards his own later days, Watson has nothing to say, either in *The Second Stain* or elsewhere. Presumably, he continued to reside in London for a little while longer after Holmes' retirement and then he too answered the call of some quiet country spot.[51] Wherever he lived, one may feel reasonably sure that his days were never dull, since he could summon to mind at will any number of glowing memories of the time when he had breathed that heady atmosphere of ever-imminent peril and high adventure which invested the presence of his friend. Yet it was not like the old days. Then his greatest pleasure, next to participating in Holmes' cases, had consisted in writing about them, and in his excursions into literary composition he had taken no little pride. Therefore, it is to be doubted that he was completely happy as long as Sherlock's severe injunction stayed his pen, however numerous his fond memories of their long association may have been. How he succeeded finally in overcoming Holmes' objections to further publicity one can only surmise, yet overcome them he did, to be permitted once again to reminisce with his pen.

Thus it came about that in 1908, after a period of some three and one-half years when there were no tangible reasons for anyone to assume that Watson had not told his last tale of the master's doings, this latter-day Boswell again broke the silence and during the next five years released in rather sporadic fashion a series of six short revelations which were later augmented by the account of the war service of Sherlock Holmes set down by an unknown hand.

Now certain critics have professed to find in these tales what to them seem to be evidences of a waning of the great Sherlock's powers, a weakening of his grasp of the principles of detection, and these same critics have proceeded to make a great to-do about the matter. It must be given them to understand, however, that of the adventures recounted in this series of tales one took place in the days before Holmes' hegira, five are of that period when he reputedly was at the height of his powers, and the seventh, which, so far as the records go, actually was his final problem, befell him when he was sixty; and regarding this last adventure it must further be noted that in the account of it, which is not of Watson's telling, there is no mention whatsoever of the necessarily brilliant use that Holmes had to make of his powers of detection in order to bring about the breakup of the German espionage ring and the capture of its chief agent Von Bork.

Various dabblers in the so-called higher criticism have also pointed out in these stories the presence of many of the inconsistencies that may be found in all revealed writings. With these critics we have no concern here except to remark that not so many years ago there was a very personable fellow going up and down the earth expatiating quite plausibly on the mistakes that Moses was supposed to have committed in his writings. Yet Moses still seems to be holding his own fairly well with his Pentateuch; and even though it is not given all inspired writers to continue to the end with eye undimmed and natural force unabated, there can be no doubt that Watson's works, despite all the efforts of his detractors, and despite the fact that his memory never was too dependable at any time, will not fare any worse than those of Moses have. In any event, persons of discernment will go on reading what both of them have written and be very grateful for the privilege.

When the first of these later Watsonian revelations became available for publication, the great Sidney Paget was dead. The art director of *The Strand Magazine* then inaugurated a new scheme for the pictorial interpretation of these additions to the canon. Whether this came about because of a feeling on his part that it would be impossible to find anyone capable of taking Paget's place, or because of some other reason, is not known. In any event, by the time the seven tales of the series had had publication seven different artists, namely, Arthur Twidle, Gilbert Holiday, Joseph Simpson, H. M. Brock, Alec Ball, Walter Paget, and A. Gilbert, had been commissioned to contribute to their embellishment. Twidle illustrated *Wisteria Lodge* and *The Bruce-Partington Plans*;

Holiday embellished *The Devil's Foot*; Simpson and Brock collaborated on the first installment of *The Red Circle*, the illustration of the second installment being entrusted to the second member of this duo; and Ball, Paget, and Gilbert provided the drawings for *The Disappearance of Lady Frances Carfax*, *The Dying Detective*, and *His Last Bow*, respectively. Altogether, forty-two illustrations were supplied for the seven stories, and thirty-two of them present Sherlock Holmes with such form and feature as each artist conceived him to have.

Of the thirty-two portraits created by these seven artists, the most outstanding undoubtedly is one for *The Red Circle* which has been assumed to have been done by Joseph Simpson, and that drawing actually is an impressive piece of work.[52] Some of Twidle's efforts also are worthy of being placed alongside the portraits done by Sidney Paget. As for the rest, they leave something to be desired. The thing that strikes one most forcibly about them is that their makers missed a great opportunity. It is true that in their pictures they have given Holmes the aquilinity that is evident in Paget's later drawings, but not one of these seven artists delineated Holmes in his deerstalker, and in overlooking that distinctive piece of headgear they missed an element that would have strengthened their portraiture to no inconsiderable degree. Admittedly, Simpson and Twidle achieved very notable results without it, but it is only necessary to compare Paget's work for the latter part of *The Hound of the Baskervilles* with the best drawings he did for *The Return of Sherlock Holmes* to perceive the vast difference that the presence of the fore-and-after made in his portraiture.

This new series of stories, together with *The Cardboard Box,* suppressed since 1894, became the volume known as *His Last Bow,* published by John Murray, London, 1917. There were no illustrations, a sad commentary on the decline that commercial bookmaking had undergone in England since the days when *The Adventures* and *The Memoirs* were placed between covers by George Newnes with all the *Strand* illustrations.

* * * * * *

The numerous changes in the line of the English aspirants to the place left vacant by Sidney Paget's passing were productive of several fine portraits, but they still left the question of succession unsettled. In America, however, there was no doubt about the succession. When the first story of the series comprising *His Last Bow* became available for release here, it was to the greatest of Sherlockian portraitists, Frederic Dorr Steele, that *Collier's* entrusted the pictorial interpretation; and like one who is undisputed master in a domain which he has made particularly his own, Steele proceeded to the continuation of his work as if there had been no three and one-half year interruption in the flow of Watson's stories.

Since *The Red Circle* and *The Devil's Foot* had their first American appearances in the American edition of *The Strand Magazine*, Steele lost the opportunity to illustrate them. But the other five stories all came to his hand for artistic decoration. *Collier's* printed only four of these tales, *The Disappearance of Lady Frances Carfax* having been secured by *The American Magazine* for publication in its columns. In the twenty-four drawings, including fourteen portraying Holmes, that Steele made for the text of these five stories he proved that his hand had lost none of its cunning. All of them are fine, durable Steele, done in the style that he seems to have developed for, and used only in, the embellishment of the canon. Some of them deserve separate mention, but as was the case with the portraits for the stories of *The Return*, it is in the cover drawings that Steele excelled, and of these alone some brief notice will be taken.

On the cover of the Sherlock Holmes number of *Collier's,* dated August 15, 1908, in which *Wisteria Lodge* was printed in advance of its publication in *The Strand Magazine*, is an unusually fine portrait study. From the nature of the pose it would seem that in all probability Steele used for his groundwork a stage photograph of William Gillette. Holmes is smoking a meditative pipe while considering the strange experience of Mr. John Scott Eccles in the house of Mr. Aloysius Garcia near Esher. The hideous face of the San Pedro mulatto peering in at the window adds a touch of the macabre to the drawing, but its presence there is a departure on Steele's part from the letter of Watson's text, since Holmes and the voodoo-worshipper never came so near to each other. In other words, the drawing is superb Holmesian portraiture but not good Watson. (See following page.)

The absence of a Sherlock Holmes portrait from the cover of the issue of *Collier's* containing *The Bruce-Partington*

Sherlock Holmes *Number*

SHERLOCK HOLMES in

Plans is more than offset by the drawing Steele produced for the cover of the issue of *The American Magazine* for December, 1911, in which *The Disappearance of Lady Frances Carfax* was printed. This fine close-up profile portrait in color, made more fetching by the deerstalker, undoubtedly was another adaptation from one of the stage photographs of William Gillette in the *rôle* of Sherlock Holmes. Steele made no attempt here to relate the portrait to the text of the story, and consequently it is not illustrative of any incident therein. However, the excellence of its composition is such as to make it of infinitely greater interest than any of the drawings provided by Steele for the illustration of the text.

Among the many pictures that Steele made for the decoration of the canon there are indeed few, if any, in which he achieved a more realistic effect than that he produced in his drawing for the cover of *Collier's* containing *The Dying Detective*. This study of Holmes feigning fatal illness is a masterpiece in its reflection of his incomparable histrionic gifts. (See next page.) Here are captured with amazing fidelity the wasted

"The Adventure of the Dying Detective"

A NEW SHERLOCK HOLMES STORY

By Sir A. Conan Doyle

look upon the long, gaunt face, the fevered glow in the great staring eyes, and the hectic flush on the hollow cheeks, all of which Holmes had simulated so convincingly that Watson, upon responding to Mrs. Hudson's call on behalf of her lodger, beheld what he thought was "indeed a deplorable spectacle." The good doctor's grave concern for Holmes' welfare is no more moving than Frederic Dorr Steele's masterly depiction of the detective's seemingly pitiful plight.

The Dying Detective was printed separately for the Advertising Department of *Collier's* and distributed as a Christmas keepsake in December, 1913. Reproduced as frontispiece was the cover drawing Steele had made for the issue of *Collier's* that contained *The Norwood Builder,* with a likeness of Dr. Watson's literary agent substituted for the handprint on the wall. It is known from Steele's own statement that he drew the original as a suggestion of what one might expect

to find upon the walls of 221B. This adaptation may be taken as a tribute to Watson's mentor in literary matters. In fact, if such drawing ever did hang upon the walls of 221B, one may feel sure it was there because the good doctor had commissioned its execution for just that purpose. His choice of artist certainly could not have been a happier one.

The cover drawing of the September 22, 1917, issue of *Collier's*, in which *His Last Bow* was published, is Steele's portrayal of Holmes as the artist imagined him to have looked in the person of Altamont. (See next page.) Now the chronicler of this tale of the detective's war service states that the nature of his disguise was such as to convey to the beholder the impression of a general resemblance to the caricature of Uncle Sam. If Steele did attempt to picture Holmes

Collier's

THE NATIONAL WEEKLY

5 cents a copy· September 22. 1917

Notice to Reader: When you finish reading this magazine place a 1-cent stamp on this notice, hand same to any postal employee and it will be placed in the hands of our soldiers or sailors at the front. No wrapping no address. A. S. BURLESON, Postmaster General

A NEW SHERLOCK HOLMES STORY by A. CONAN DOYLE

SHERLOCK HOLMES in

thus, the effort was not a wholehearted one. As much may be surmised from the fact that he drew him cradling his chin in his hand in such a manner that the most telling element in his disguise, the "horrible goatee," is hidden from view. Perhaps Steele felt too kindly toward the detective to subject him to travesty here. In any case, the cap Holmes wears, his long shock of hair, and his clear-cut aquiline features all combine to give him an aspect that carries just a little too much dignity to be even faintly comical.

In America, the stories were collected as in the English edition put out by John Murray and published under the same title by the George H. Doran Company. There were no illustrations.

* * * * * * *

It must ever redound to Watson's fame that when the release of the preceding series of short stories. had come to a halt temporarily after the magazine publication of *The Dying Detective*, he sought and secured Holmes' permission to record the strange and terrible circumstances connected with the case known as *The Valley of Fear*, the fourth and the last of the longer revelations. The account of this case, in many ways the weirdest and the most appalling of those that came to Holmes out of an American background, had publication in *The Strand Magazine* in nine installments, beginning with the September, 1914, number. As a result of the arrangements made for its illustration, the name of yet another artist, Frank Wiles, was added to the lengthening list of those who have had to do with the iconography of Sherlock Holmes. His drawings run to thirty-one in number, including fifteen in which there are presentments of the great detective. These contain some passably good Holmesian portraiture. On the whole, it is not as good as the best of the drawings for *The Strand Magazine* appearances of *His Last Bow,* and certainly not the equal of Paget's work for *The Return of Sherlock Holmes*, but still considerably above the average level of the attainments of Paget's other successors. Wiles' very first drawing, done in color and used as frontispiece to the initial installment, is by far his finest effort toward the pictorial interpretation of *The Valley of Fear*.[53] This study of Holmes exerting all his powers of concentration on the solution of Fred Porlock's cipher, for which at the last moment that pseudonymous minion of Professor Moriarty had failed to provide the key, is of itself sufficiently convincing evidence that Wiles had more than a mere superficial insight into the appearance, manners, and characteristics of the man he was delineating. This portrait excels Wiles' other depictions of Holmes in much the same way that Steele's cover portraits surpass his textual representations. If Wiles had not made another drawing for *The Valley of Fear*, he would still have to be given credit for a notable contribution to the portraiture of Sherlock Holmes.

The Valley of Fear was published as a book in England by Smith, Elder & Company in 1915, with one illustration by Wiles.

* * * * * *

In America, *The Valley of Fear* was first presented to the public through the pages of *The Sunday Magazine*, in serial form. It appeared in ten installments, printed in the numbers published from September 22 to November 20, 1914, and was embellished with eleven illustrations executed by Arthur I. Keller, one of the better known magazine artists of the day. Five of his drawings mirror his mental image of Sherlock. There may be just a suggestion of the Steele influence in his portraits, but certainly not enough to make them distinguished. Keller was short on interpretative qualities and achieved his effects mainly by delineating his chief subject in exaggerated postures and extremes of sartorial splendor. For all his love of dramatic situations, and *The Valley of Fear* has many of them, Holmes never was quite the poseur that Keller depicts. The portraits call to mind those done in the early days by W. H. Hyde, whose emphasis was on costume, at the expense of characterization.

The text of *The Valley of Fear,* when produced in book form in America by the George H. Doran Company, was accompanied by seven of Keller's magazine drawings, reproduced on greatly reduced scale.

* * * * * *

Twice the flow of Watson's revelations seemed to have been terminated, and yet neither in *The Final Problem* nor in *The Second Stain* did the good doctor write *finis* to the adventures of Sherlock Holmes. For a time it appeared as though *His Last Bow* was to be the third and absolutely final attempt to bring the saga to a close. But there was still more to come, twelve more of the shorter revelations. Nine of them are attributable to Watson, two were by Holmes himself, and one was set down by an unknown hand.

The publication of this concluding series of tales began with the appearance of *The Mazarin Stone* in the October, 1921, number of *The Strand Magazine*. Although Watson did not record this adventure, it must be assumed to have been based on material supplied from his notebook, for he was present and took some small part in the recovery of the stolen gem.

A. Gilbert was again called upon, and he illustrated *The Mazarin Stone* and *Thor Bridge*, and thereafter the mark of his hand is seen no more in the pictorial interpretation of the canon. The illustration of further emissions was then entrusted for a time to Howard Elcock, and for *The Creeping Man*, *The Sussex Vampire*, *The Three Garridebs*, *The Illustrious Client*, *The Three Gables*, *The Blanched Soldier*, and *The Lion's Mane* he did thirty-four drawings, including twenty-seven in which Holmes appears. Though hardly distinguished, Elcock's portraiture for the most part is competent in execution.

For the illustration of the last three revelations, namely, *The Retired Colourman*, *The Veiled Lodger*, and *Shoscombe Old Place*, in the order of their publication, the art director of *The Strand Magazine* engaged Frank Wiles, the artist who had made the drawings for *The Valley of Fear* some twelve years previously. His thirteen drawings include ten portraits of Holmes. Among these are some profiles that bear comparison with the best efforts attained by the other English artists who came after Sidney Paget, but, as with Elcock's drawings, it would not be practical to consider any of them in detail. However, Wiles' work for the final story, *Shoscombe Old Place,* does deserve particular mention because of the fact that in three of the illustrations the deerstalker reappears in *The Strand Magazine* for the first time since the stories of *The Return* were published there. The best of these shows Holmes with lantern in hand examining the ancient chapel crypt of the Falder baronets.[54] While the scene depicted is far from being a cheerful one, Sherlockians are able to entertain the pleasant thought that in his final *Strand* appearance Holmes made his exit wearing his deerstalker.

The aforementioned twelve stories were published by John Murray in book form as *The Case-Book of Sherlock Holmes*, London, 1927, without illustrations.

* * * * * *

The initial American releases of the stories comprising *The Case-Book* were made in three different magazines. *Hearst's International* published the first four, the embellishment of which was entrusted to three illustrators. Frederic Dorr Steele did the drawings for *The Mazarin Stone* and *The Creeping Man*; G. Patrick Nelson supplied those for *Thor Bridge*; and W. T. Benda illustrated *The Sussex Vampire*. Unfortunately, no one seems to have taken any thought to provide lavish drawings in color such as those that once brightened the front covers of *Collier's*. Steele presented Holmes in each of the four illustrations he provided for *The Mazarin Stone* issue (November, 1921), and in three of the seven for *The Creeping Man* issue (March, 1923). He maintained his usual high level of performance in these drawings, among which profiles predominate, but in none of them does he contribute anything startlingly novel to Holmesian portraiture, not even in that one which shows the bust of the detective fashioned in wax by Tavernier, the French modeler. It will be recalled that this was the second time Steele had delineated the detective in effigy. Holmes called the bust "a pretty little thing," but Sam Merton paid its maker a higher compliment when, at sight of it, he exclaimed, "Well, strike me! Madame Tussaud ain't in it. It's the living spit of him, gown and all." This remark must be accepted as evidence that the Tussaud establishment, once located in Baker Street, had a wax effigy of the famous criminologist on display, and that it was greatly inferior to Tavernier's model. The Tussaud bust could hardly have been the one made by Oscar Meunier, through which Colonel Sebastian Moran put a bullet at the time of the case of *The Empty House,* for that bust was a masterpiece in wax.

The Mazarin Stone probably was the very last case Holmes solved at 221B Baker Street before retiring from active practice. Consequently, the small portrait study of a very resolute Holmes informing Count Sylvius that he wanted

"that yellow diamond," the Mazarin stone, may well have been the final portrayal of him in his old quarters. In any case, it calls for reproduction here.

G. Patrick Nelson's seven drawings for *Thor Bridge*, in the February and March, 1922, issues of *Hearst's International*, include three which picture Holmes, and these portray the detective very much after Steele's pattern. Indeed, it may be said that, if Steele did exert any considerable influence on American portrayers of Holmes, Nelson is the only

one whose work strongly reflects that influence. His portrayals of Holmes' head are so much like Steele's that, without identifying signatures, it would be difficult to distinguish between them. His study of Holmes examining the stonework of the bridge at Thor Place after concluding his experiment with Watson's revolver is an exceptionally striking one, made so to no little degree by the deerstalker with which the artist had the good sense to cover the detective. In fact,

SHERLOCK HOLMES in

the study is so good that it deserves reproduction. It will be noted that the portrait is more clear-cut than those by Steele for the text of Watson's final revelations.

Two of the four illustrations which W. T. Benda made for *The Sussex Vampire* issue of *Hearst's International* (January, 1924), contain his conceptions of Holmes' appearance. The portraits are not quite worthy of this artist, who was noted for the strange masklike expressions with which he invested the faces of his subjects. This singular feature of his work is present here, but one cannot escape the conviction that Benda really failed to grasp the opportunity to make an outstanding contribution to Holmesian portraiture when he gave the masklike face to Robert Ferguson instead of to Holmes, who is made to appear as being monstrously beaked, with receding forehead and scarcely any chin at all. In view of this fact, it seems advisable to leave Benda's conceptions of the detective buried in the pages of the magazine in which they came off so badly.

The same courtesy should be accorded to John Richard Flanagan's efforts to portray Holmes in his embellishments of *The Three Garridebs* and *The Illustrious Client*, which were published by *Collier's* in the October 25, 1924, and the November 8, 1924, issues respectively. The truth of the matter is that Flanagan, otherwise a highly competent draughtsman, had no flair at all for Holmesian portraiture. In his illustrations for the two stories he included his pictorial ideas of the detective's appearance three times.

In the year following the initial publication of *The Sussex Vampire*, *The Illustrious Client*, and *The Three Garridebs*, these three stories, and *The Creeping Man*, were reprinted in the Sunday section of *The Courier-Journal* of Louisville. Steele was commissioned to provide illustrations, one large-size drawing for each story. Those for the first three named above include portraits of Holmes. However, none of them adds anything to Steele's already secure laurels or makes any outstanding new contribution to Holmesian portraiture. The circumstance is worthy of note mainly for the fact that thus Steele was enabled to illustrate all the short revelations beginning with *The Empty House* except *The Red Circle* and *The Devil's Foot,* which were printed in the American edition of *The Strand Magazine*, with the drawings made by the English artists.

SHERLOCK HOLMES in

The last six stories of *The Case Book* were released in various numbers of *Liberty* from September 18, 1926, to March 5, 1927. By a happy inspiration, the art editor of that magazine engaged Steele to do the illustrations and so enabled the artist to whom Holmes owes his most sympathetic and most satisfying interpretation in pictorial art to round out his graphic exposition of the detective in his closing American appearances. But again it is a matter for regret that no provisions were made for cover drawings. For the text of the six stories Steele executed thirty-four drawings, half of which contain portraits of Holmes. A certain amount of interest attaches to all of them because of their subject, but for our purposes it suffices to turn more than a loving glance to only two or three of the seventeen.

Among them is the only Steele drawing for the series of stories comprising *The Case Book* that approaches what may be termed his grand manner of portraying Holmes: the large one he executed for *The Lion's Mane*, which depicts the retired detective as he stood, a lonely figure against the sombre background of the Sussex coast, meditating upon the strange occurrences that had taken place there and trying to riddle the mysterious circumstances under which Fitzroy McPherson and his dog had come to horrible ends. (Opposite page.) If the drawing had been done in color, with the figure of Holmes presented on larger scale, it would compare favorably with the famous cover drawings Steele made for *Collier's* during the time when the stories of *The Return* and *His Last Bow* were appearing in that magazine.

The same may be said of the drawing made especially by Steele for *The Courier-Journal* in 1927 when *The Blanched Soldier* was reprinted in that newspaper. Incidentally, this piece of work is another example of the liberties Steele occasionally took with the exact wording of the canon. Among the drawings he had provided for *Collier's* printing of the story was one which illustrated the scene in which Mr. James Dodd, at Tuxbury Old Park, actually saw the pale and ghastly face of Godfrey Emsworth "glimmering as white as a cheese in the darkness." The present drawing, then, is not according to the letter of Watson's text. Holmes, in dressing gown, meditating upon Mr. Dodd's problem, is not at Tuxbury Old Park, but in Baker Street. Is the blotched and mottled face of Emsworth in the drawing a materialization of that which

Mr. Dodd had described as appearing to him out of the night at Tuxbury Old Park? Perhaps Steele was intimating that Holmes did possess powers that were above and beyond the natural.[55]

With the publication of *The Retired Colourman*, *The Veiled Lodger*, and *Shoscombe Old Place* Watson wrote *finis* to the canon, and there is no more fitting way to bring to a close this sketchy consideration of the Holmesian portraits of Frederic Dorr Steele, incomparable portrayer of the great fathomer, than to call attention to one of the drawings for *Shoscombe Old Place*, Watson's very last revelation. It is a superb little study of the great man, who sits with pipe in hand and microscope before him. Presumably it portrays him at the moment before he straightened up and in triumphant tone of voice announced, "It is glue, Watson. . . . Unquestionably it is glue." Whether or not the finding caused the accused man in the St. Pancras case to hang we shall never know, but this much we can say with unhesitant certainty when viewing this or any other Frederic Dorr Steele portrayal of the protagonist of the canon: "It is Sherlock Holmes, sir. . . . Unquestionably it is Mr. Sherlock Holmes."[56]

Notes

[1] *A Study in Scarlet*, chap. ii.

[2] In 1914, it is stated in *His Last Bow*, Holmes was sixty, which would make 1854 the year of his birth. Therefore, in 1881 he was twenty-seven. Watson is generally supposed to have been about a year older than Holmes. See "On the Period of Holmes's Active Practice," in H. W. Bell's *Sherlock Holmes and Dr. Watson, the Chronology of their Adventures.*

[3] One who, next to Watson, probably enjoyed the closest personal acquaintanceship with Holmes, and undoubtedly had as affectionate a place for him in his heart and as exact an image of him in his mind, is authority for this revealing sidelight on the detective's facial aspect. Commenting on the work of Sidney Paget, one of Holmes' early portrayers, A. Conan Doyle stated that the detective "was a more beaky-nosed, hawk-faced man, approaching more to the Red Indian type," than that artist had pictured him.— "Conan Doyle Tells the True Story of Sherlock Holmes," *Tit-bits*, December 15, 1900.

[4] *The Hound of the Baskervilles,* chap. i. Dr. Mortimer was deeply impressed by Holmes' supra-orbital development. On the other hand, Professor Moriarty found that the detective had "less frontal development" than he had expected.—*The Final Problem.*

[5] *The Sign of the Four*, chap. i. There is no mention of any illustrations. All subsequent editions of *A Study in Scarlet* are designated as "being a reprint from the reminiscences of John H. Watson, M.D., late of the Army Medical Department."

[6] That was to come a little later. "Your pictures are not unlike you, sir," said James Winter, alias Morecroft, alias Killer Evans, alias John Garrideb. In view of the pronounced dissimilarity of many of Holmes' portraits appearing in the illustrations made for Watson's stories, Garrideb's statement must be taken as referring to newspaper publications of the detective's likenesses.

[7] So far, the cases of which we have accounts were:

The Gloria Scott—Summer-Autumn, 1875; The Musgrave Ritual—September, 1878; A Study in Scarlet—March, 1881; Silver Blaze—early Autumn, 1881; The Beryl Coronet—February, 1882; The Yellow Face—April, 1882; The Speckled Band—April, 1883; Charles Augustus Milverton—February, 1884; The Cardboard Box—August, 1885; and The Hound of the Baskervilles— September-October,1886.

And of further recorded cases in which Holmes had a hand between the time of the publishers' acceptance of *A Study in Scarlet* and the date of its publication, there were The Valley of Fear—January, 1887; The Reigate Puzzle—April, 1887; The Sign of the Four—September, 1887; The Noble Bachelor —October, 1887; and The Resident Patient—late October, 1887.

The dating throughout is that which has been verified or, where incorrectly stated or wanting in the text, established by H. W. Bell in his *Sherlock Holmes and Dr. Watson.*

[8] *The Echo* of March 11, 1881 (*A Study in Scarlet,* chap. vii), and *The Standard* of September 28, 1887 (*The Sign of the Four,* chap. viii), contain mention of Holmes' name in connection with cases in which the official forces were concerned. In neither instance does he receive full credit. That he could hope to have attributed to him only in cases where the official forces had not been called in and he was working entirely on his own. One such case is mentioned in the opening paragraph of *The Reigate Puzzle.* Others of a similar nature which followed shortly are listed in *A Scandal in Bohemia.*

[9] The word "Rache," written at eye level by Hope, who was not much under six and a half feet tall, stands just a little above Holmes' own eyes.

[10] *The Musgrave Ritual.*

[11] "'Old woman be damned!' said Sherlock Holmes." Jefferson Hope carried the secret of this person's identity with him to his grave. His unknown accomplice had a knowledge of London as thorough and as exact as Holmes' own.

[12] See photograph in *Life* v. 16, no. 18, p. 82.

[13] *The Sign of the Four*, chap. viii.

[14] *Memories and Adventures*, Hodder and Stoughton, London [1924].

[15] A Holmes of similar visage, set in highly determined cast, is seen in the frontispiece to this edition, which pictures him assisting Lestrade in the taking of Jefferson Hope.

[16] The good doctor twice makes mention of Holmes' Indian-like composure; once, in *The Naval Treaty,* and again, in *The Crooked Man*. See note 3.

[17] *The Baker Street Journal*, v. 2, no. 1, p. 105.

[18] Lately, steps have been taken in certain quarters to disprove that such relationship ever existed between Doyle and Watson, but to little or no avail. Doyle openly admitted the arrangement in the preface to *His Last Bow*. He no doubt assisted also in getting Holmes' two stories, *The Blanched Soldier* and *The Lion's Mane*, published in *The Strand Magazine*.

[19] The first twelve adventures appeared in *The Strand Magazine* from July, 1891, to June, 1892; the second twelve, in the same periodical, from December, 1892, to December, 1893. These adventures occurred over a period of sixteen years that began with Holmes' first case, in 1875, and ended with what was supposed for a time to have been his final problem, in 1891.

[20] Walter Paget, also an artist, is best remembered perhaps for his illustrations for the story of another great adventurer, Robinson Crusoe. After Sidney's death, Walter did the illustrations for the *Strand* appearance of *The Dying Detective*.

[21] All of these drawings were reproduced in *The Adventures* as published in book form by George Newnes, London, 1892.

[22] Since *The Cardboard Box* was not included when the second series of the adventures was put into book form by George Newnes in 1894, only ninety of the *Strand* illustrations were reproduced. One of them, however, had originally been made for *The Cardboard Box*. It was used to embellish the opening paragraphs of *The Resident Patient*, which, in the revised form in which they appeared in the book, were much the same as the introductory part of *The Cardboard Box*.

[23] At least one example of the work of each of these various engravers is included in the illustrations reproduced herein.

[24] Two of Swain's engravings are reproduced in the text, one above and one lower left, page 29. Hare's engraving is at top of page 25.

[25] Similar descriptions occur in *The Red-Headed League* and *The Hound of the Baskervilles*, chap. ii.

[26] See, also, *The Devil's Foot* and *The Creeping Man*.

[27] In *The Hound of the Baskervilles*, chap. iii, Watson relates that upon his return to Baker Street from a day at his club, the first impression he received as he opened the door of the sitting room at 221B was that a fire had broken out there, for the atmosphere was so heavy that the light of the lamp on the table was almost obscured by it. Upon closer examination, however, Watson perceived that it was only the acrid fumes of Holmes' favorite brand of shag tobacco, that is, the strongest kind.

[28] *A Case of Identity.*

[29] *The Engineer's Thumb.*

[30] *The Sign of the Four*, chap. i.

[31] *The Yellow Face.*

[32] *A Scandal in Bohemia.*

[33] *Black Peter.*

[34] *The Red-Headed League.* Athelney Jones paid Holmes a fine compliment on his acting in *The Sign of the Four,* chap. ix. Baron Dowson also testified to his histrionic ability when he said, the night before his neck was stretched by due process of law, that what the law had gained the stage had lost.— *The Mazarin Stone.*

[35] See also *The Bruce-Partington Plans.*

[36] Chap. iii.

[37] Chap. vi.

[38] Emile-Jean-Horace Vernet, 1789-1863.

[39] Carl W. Drepperd, *American Pioneer Arts and Artists*, p. 123. The late Mr. Drepperd had in his possession a signed chalk portrait, upon the matting of which was written, "Study by Horace Vernet, 1847, for Charles Henry Fisher, Charleston, S.C. First lesson in drawing."

[40] *The Final Problem* was published in *The Strand Magazine* for December, 1893. Holmes returned early in April, 1894.

[41] *The Times-Star* did not use a single illustration with the four stories that appeared in that newspaper, and *The Courier-Journal* did not avail itself of any of the drawings provided by the syndicate until it printed *Adventures of Five Orange Pips,* and thereafter omitted them from two of the other five stories that followed.

[42] In connection with his published photograph, as stated in *The Three Garridebs.*

43 This delineation has been reproduced so often that it hardly seems necessary to include it here.

44 The American edition of *The Strand Magazine*, dated one month later than the English edition, was published continuously from January, 1891, to February, 1916, when it was discontinued. The only other Holmes stories to appear in its pages were *The Red Circle* and *The Devil's Foot*.

45 After ten weekly installments had appeared, the story was brought to its conclusion in the next seven issues of *The Courier-Journal*, without illustrations.

46 Harold J. Shepstone, "William Gillette as Sherlock Holmes," *The Strand Magazine*, December, 1901.

47 Frederic Dorr Steele, "Sherlock Holmes in Pictures," *The New Yorker*, May 22, 1937.

48 Frederic Dorr Steele, "My First Meeting with Sherlock Holmes," *The Baker Street Journal*, v. 4, no. 1.

49 Ellery Queen, forematter to Frederic Dorr Steele's parody, "The Adventure of the Murdered Art Editor."

50 It is possible, of course, that P. F. Collier & Son had other plans for the use of these drawings that precluded their availability to McClure, Phillips and Company. Several of them were inserted in *A Study in Scarlet and other Stories* and *The Sign of the Four and other Stories*, the first two volumes in Collier's three-volume Sherlock Holmes edition, New York, no date, with captions designed to make their presence there seem warrantable. However, it is evident to anyone familiar with the drawings that they do not belong there and are, for the most part, inapposite. The same cannot be said of the one new illustration supplied by Steele for the further embellishment of *A Study in Scarlet*, a drawing which presents a youthful-looking Holmes examing the word "Rache" with a small magnifying glass.

51 *His Last Bow*.

52 *The Strand Magazine*, March, 1911. This drawing was reproduced in *The New York Times*, 7 : 1, April 2, 1944.

53 *The Strand Magazine*, September, 1914.

54 *The Strand Magazine*, April, 1927.

55 *The Courier-Journal* also reprinted *The Three Gables* and *The Lion's Mane* in 1927, both with drawings by Steele that depict scenes he had delineated in his illustrations done for the same stories when they appeared in *Liberty*. In their redrawn form for *The Courier-Journal* they present some noticeable changes in detail.

56 It will be noted that in the American edition of *The Case Book of Sherlock Holmes*, issued by the George H. Doran Company in 1927 without illustrations, the stories are not presented in the order of their magazine appearances.

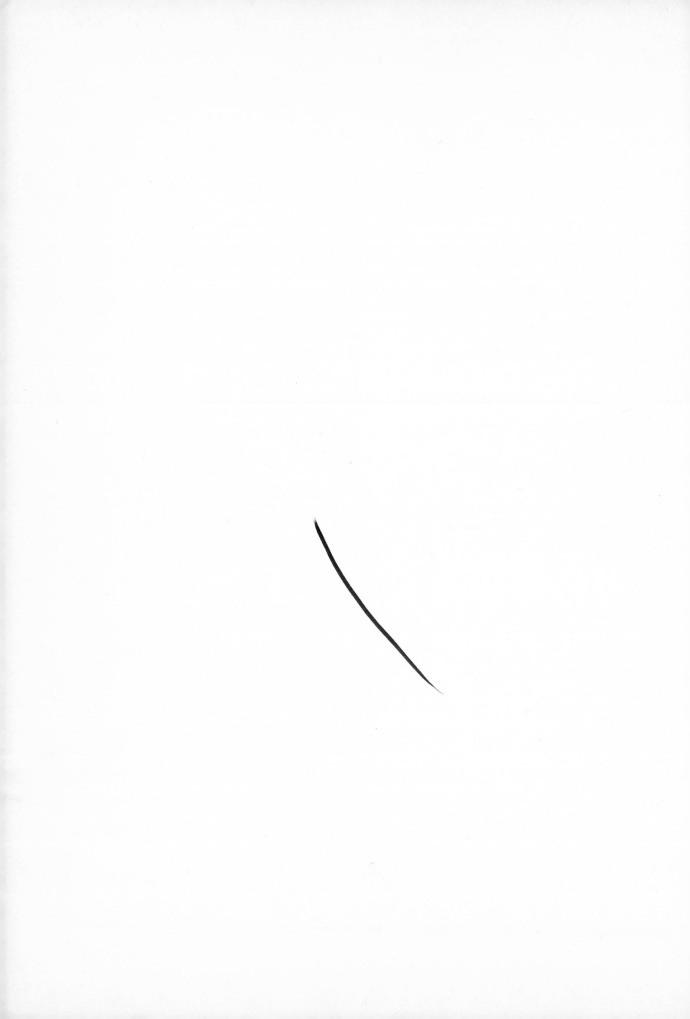

Index

NOTE: *Page numbers in italic type indicate illustrations reproduced in this book.*

SHERLOCK HOLMES in